Editor
Gisela Lee

Managing Editor
Karen Goldfluss, M.S. Ed.

Editor-in-Chief
Sharon Coan, M.S. Ed.

Cover Artist
Brenda DiAntonis

Art Coordinator
Kevin Barnes

Imaging
Rosa C. See
Temo Parra

Product Manager
Phil Garcia

Publisher
Mary D. Smith, M.S. Ed.

Presidential Puzzlers

Ages 8–12

Author

Diane Marshall

Teacher Created Resources, Inc.
6421 Industry Way
Westminster, CA 92683
www.teachercreated.com
ISBN-0-7439-3353-2
©*2002 Teacher Created Resources, Inc.*
Reprinted, 2005
Made in U.S.A.

Table of Contents

Table of Contents *(cont.)*

Presidential Puzzlers is a useful book for teachers and parents which combines reading, math, and social studies skills with interesting information about our presidents. The book is divided into three sections: Reading, Math, and Social Studies. Each section contains several different types of puzzles that students must solve in order to find out different facts about some of the presidents. Some of these puzzles include:

- word searches
- fill-ins
- crossword puzzles
- cryptograms
- brain teasers
- riddles

This book is designed for students ages 8–12, but can be used at other levels also. The activities in this book can be used as time-fillers, remediation activities for older students, re-teaching or review activities, and research assignments.

Presidential Puzzlers allows students to practice basic and advanced skills while enjoying the challenge of solving puzzles and finding out little known information about past and current presidents.

Listed below is an index of the presidents and the pages where you can find activities about them. (**Note:** Not all presidents are listed since only some were used for the activities in this book.)

Presidential Index

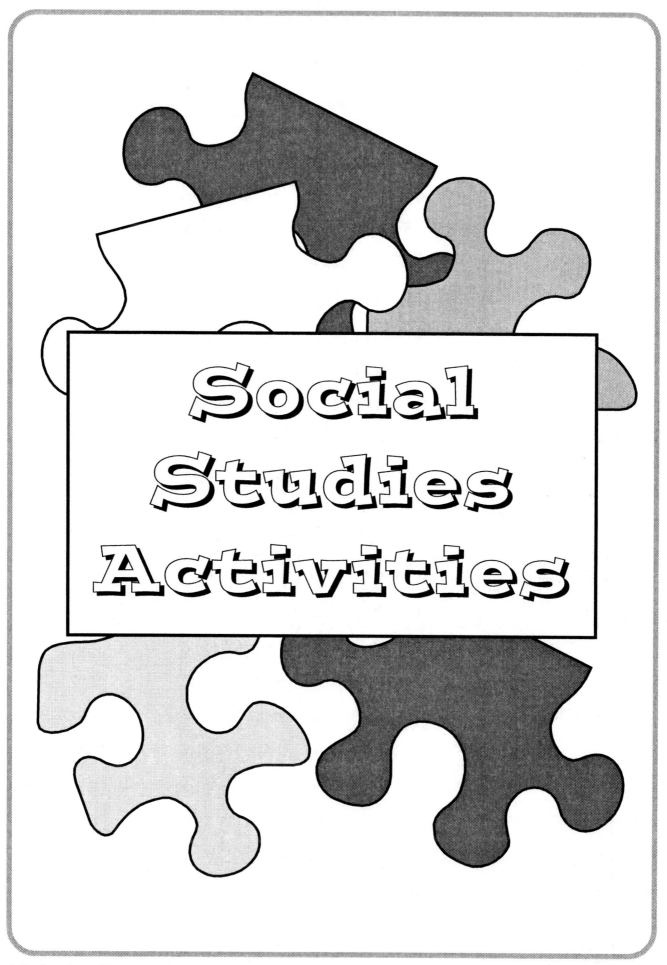

Social Studies Activities

Listed below are all of the men who have served as the President of the United States and the dates they served in office.

1. George Washington	1789–1797	23. Benjamin Harrison	1889–1893
2. John Adams	1797–1801	24. Grover Cleveland	1893–1897
3. Thomas Jefferson	1801–1809	25. William McKinley	1897–1901
4. James Madison	1809–1817	26. Theodore Roosevelt	1901–1909
5. James Monroe	1817–1825	27. William H. Taft	1909–1913
6. John Quincy Adams	1825–1829	28. Woodrow Wilson	1913–1921
7. Andrew Jackson	1829–1837	29. Warren G. Harding	1921–1923
8. Martin Van Buren	1837–1841	30. Calvin Coolidge	1923–1929
9. William H. Harrison	1841	31. Herbert Hoover	1929–1933
10. John Tyler	1841–1845	32. Franklin D. Roosevelt	1933–1945
11. James K. Polk	1845–1849	33. Harry Truman	1945–1953
12. Zachary Taylor	1849–1850	34. Dwight Eisenhower	1953–1961
13. Millard Fillmore	1850–1853	35. John F. Kennedy	1961–1963
14. Franklin Pierce	1853–1857	36. Lyndon Johnson	1963–1969
15. James Buchanan	1857–1861	37. Richard Nixon	1969–1974
16. Abraham Lincoln	1861–1865	38. Gerald Ford	1974–1977
17. Andrew Johnson	1865–1869	39. Jimmy Carter	1977–1981
18. Ulysses S. Grant	1869–1877	40. Ronald Reagan	1981–1989
19. Rutherford B. Hayes	1877–1881	41. George Bush	1989–1993
20. James A. Garfield	1881	42. Bill Clinton	1993–2001
21. Chester A. Arthur	1881–1885	43. George W. Bush	2001–
22. Grover Cleveland	1885–1889		

Find the Presidents

Use the list of presidents on page 6 to find all of their names in this word search. Look only for their last names. If two presidents had the same last name, it will be in the puzzle twice. If the same man was president more than once, his name is only in the puzzle one time.

```
A S M D H F Y L X M N O T N I L C T D I V E G K Y
Z N K E N N E D Y U K G N I D R A H S R Q F B D U
S O J N X T T O R O W T C Z R Y D N E E D W P F T
M S Z O X J H M A A U V M V L D G A O V Y L Y A T
A I X S P H C O S O D V V O T Z G T Q S P A F U E
D D O L P N A H O H R R R L W A T L S I K T H O E
A A X I W W I R F V A J E H N O R I O J U C R V J
E M O W Q N C G R T E V Z H Z H U N T L I N A D X
R G T O G P R G C I E R E F U S M C Z B O B R J S
O T D T Y A K A G S S X L H Q U A O F M R P E Y W
M R O M N F L W O V Q O W L S B N L I N E I T L D
L N M T K L O O G O Z O N B L U C N V M W E R K N
L M F W Z A R R F Y V K C E B X B H X E O R A I A
I R J E F F E R S O N O S W O Z Z T G Q H C C A L
F F K J W D W P R T N P M I J M L A T J N E O D E
E H P J C X M D H O W R A G N E R D P T E Y E G V
J G D S S M I S S U N F D Z V F K D L Y S P X F E
O L D X E W C N J A P X A E I S G A I W I U G Z L
H K U I G U H K T M D U S E J H K P U A E Z V I C
N L A V L O M E I W P O L N A N A H C U B R J B Z
S W E E J O R G R N O D T M A C G P Y W J W Q U F
O E V A O S O L B R L J N B N O S I R R A H S A O
N R U H T R A C D W K E F O I N W N I X O N R G R
R C E V A N B U R E N G Y U Q R E L Y T V O A O D
```

Four American presidents have been killed while in office. Some were killed by men who were unhappy about the way the president was running the country. One was even killed merely because he refused to give the man a job. Listed below are the presidents who were assassinated in office and the men who killed them. Use their last names to fill-in the puzzle below.

- Abraham _____ was assassinated on April 15, 1865, by John Wilkes _____ while

(1 ACROSS)   (2 DOWN)

watching a play with his wife at Ford's Theater.

- James _____ was shot by Charles _____ on July 2, 1881, while walking through a

(3 ACROSS)   (3 DOWN)

train station. He died 10 weeks later.

- William _____ died on September 14, 1901, eight days after being shot

(4 ACROSS)

by Leon _____ .

(5 ACROSS)

- John F. _____ was shot and killed by Lee Harvey _____ while riding in a car down

(6 DOWN)   (7 DOWN)

a Dallas street on November 22, 1963.

The winner of the election becomes president. But what happens to the loser? In fact do we even remember who the losers are? In the activity below, match the president to his opponent.

President	Opponent
_____ 1. Theodore Roosevelt	A. George Bush
_____ 2. William Taft	B. John W. Davis
_____ 3. Benjamin Harrison	C. Aaron Burr
_____ 4. Calvin Coolidge	D. Alton Parker
_____ 5. Abraham Lincoln	E. Stephen Douglas
_____ 6. Harry S. Truman	F. Hubert Humphrey
_____ 7. Dwight D. Eisenhower	G. Thomas Dewey
_____ 8. John F. Kennedy	H. Gerald Ford
_____ 9. Thomas Jefferson	I. William Bryan
_____ 10. James K. Polk	J. Grover Cleveland
_____ 11. Andrew Jackson	K. Richard Nixon
_____ 12. Rutherford B. Hayes	L. Charles Hughes
_____ 13. Woodrow Wilson	M. Henry Clay
_____ 14. Lyndon Johnson	N. Samuel Tilden
_____ 15. Jimmy Carter	O. Walter Mondale
_____ 16. Richard Nixon	P. John Quincy Adams
_____ 17. Ronald Reagan	Q. Herbert Hoover
_____ 18. George Bush	R. Barry Goldwater
_____ 19. Franklin Roosevelt	S. Adlai Stevenson
_____ 20. Bill Clinton	T. Michael Dukakis

George W. Bush Puzzle

Use the word list at the bottom of the page to fill in the puzzle below and learn more about President George W. Bush.

Word List

Barbara	Spot	baseball team	governor
Jenna	India	Yale	Harvard
Laura	Barney	twins	

Presidential Only's

Using the presidents' last names below, fill in the puzzle by answering the clues.

Across

1. only president to serve more than two terms
2. only president to be elected twice without 50% of the popular vote
3. only president who never went to school
4. only president who was a prisoner of war
5. only unmarried president

Down

1. only president who was also vice president but not elected to either office.
2. only president to say "I promise" instead of "I swear" at inauguration
3. only president to be named a sworn enemy of the U.S.
4. only president to resign
5. only president to study medicine

Presidents

Franklin D. Roosevelt	Franklin Pierce
James Buchanan	Bill Clinton
Richard Nixon	Andrew Jackson
Gerald Ford	John Tyler
Andrew Johnson	William Henry Harrison

Presidential Cryptograms

In each of the puzzles below, each letter of the alphabet stands for another letter. You must break the code to answer each of the riddles. All of the answers will be the names of presidents. Part of the code is given below to help you get started.

Z = A	V = E	R = I	L = O	F = U

1. This president had two women attempt to assassinate him in the same month.

   ___ ___ ___ ___ ___ ___   ___ ___ ___ ___
    T   V   I   Z   O   W   U   L   I   W

2. He was the oldest man elected president.

   ___ ___ ___ ___ ___ ___   ___ ___ ___ ___ ___ ___
    I   L   M   Z   O   W   I   V   Z   T   Z   M

3. He lived most of his life with a bullet two inches away from his heart.

   ___ ___ ___ ___ ___ ___   ___ ___ ___ ___ ___ ___ ___
    Z   M   W   I   V   D   Q   Z   X   P   H   L   M

4. This president had to borrow money to go to his own inauguration.

   ___ ___ ___ ___ ___ ___   ___ ___ ___ ___ ___ ___ ___ ___ ___ ___
    T   V   L   I   T   V   D   Z   H   S   R   M   T   G   L   M

5. He was the first president to live in the White House.

   ___ ___ ___ ___   ___ ___ ___ ___ ___
    Q   L   S   M   Z   W   Z   N   H

6. He was shot in Ford's Theater.

   ___ ___ ___ ___ ___ ___ ___   ___ ___ ___ ___ ___ ___ ___
    Z   Y   I   Z   S   Z   N   O   R   M   X   L   O   M

7. This president had the most children. He had 15!

   ___ ___ ___ ___   ___ ___ ___ ___ ___
    Q   L   S   M   G   B   O   V   I

8. He was the writer of the Declaration of Independence.

   ___ ___ ___ ___ ___ ___   ___ ___ ___ ___ ___ ___ ___ ___ ___
    G   S   L   N   Z   H   Q   V   U   U   V   I   H   L   M

9. This man was president during World War I.

   ___ ___ ___ ___ ___ ___ ___   ___ ___ ___ ___ ___ ___
    D   L   L   W   I   L   D   D   R   O   H   L   M

Only a few presidents, like John Quincy Adams, have used their middle names. Several have used an initial or nothing at all, leaving us to wonder about their full names. Using the list of names below, see if you can figure out the middle names of these presidents. Some letters have been filled in for you.

1. William ___ ___ ___ R (___) Harrison

2. Franklin ___ E ___ ___ ___ (___) Roosevelt

3. Dwight ___ ___ ___ (I) ___ Eisenhower

4. John ___ ___ ___ ___ ___ (___) ___ ___ ___ D Kennedy

5. Lyndon (___) ___ I ___ ___ ___ Johnson

6. Richard ___ (I) ___ ___ ___ ___ ___ Nixon

7. James ___ A ___ (___) Carter

8. Ronald (___) ___ ___ ___ O ___ Reagan

9. George ___ ___ ___ ___ ___ ___ T   ___ ___ (___) K ___ ___ Bush

10. William ___ ___ ___ ___ ___ ___ S ___ (___) Clinton

11. Warren (___) ___ ___ ___ ___ L ___ ___ ___ Harding

12. William ___ ___ W (___) ___ ___ Taft

Names

Fitzgerald	Milhous	David	Baines
Henry	Delano	Howard	Herbert Walker
Gamaliel	Jefferson	Earl	Wilson

Now, unscramble the letters in parenthesis to finish this sentence about the president's home, the White House.

The White House includes a movie theater, an indoor swimming pool, and a

___ ___ ___ ___ ___ ___ ___ ___   ___ ___ ___ ___ ___.

Who Was First?

Find the last names of these presidents who were first in the puzzle below. The names may go across, down, or backwards.

- The first president to die in office was William Henry Harrison. He died 31 days into his term.

- Warren Harding was the first president to speak on the radio. He was also the first president to visit Canada.

- William McKinley was the first president to ride in a car. He was taken to the hospital in an electric ambulance after being shot.

- John Adams was the first president to also have a son elected president. His son John Quincy Adams was elected 24 years later.

- William Taft was the first president to own a car.

- Franklin D. Roosevelt was the first president to have a presidential aircraft. He only flew on it once.

- The first president to be born in a hospital was Jimmy Carter.

- Andrew Johnson was the first president to be impeached. He was found not guilty by only one vote.

H	R	O	O	S	E	V	E	L	T
A	C	R	B	D	U	N	C	X	P
R	T	Y	Q	H	A	M	P	L	I
R	E	R	Y	A	D	A	M	S	J
I	V	E	B	R	O	L	U	N	G
S	Z	T	Y	D	A	A	E	W	H
O	T	R	M	I	P	L	E	F	D
N	A	A	X	N	Q	T	A	F	T
B	J	C	S	G	O	K	Y	N	G
R	T	D	N	O	S	N	H	O	J
W	H	Y	D	C	V	R	S	E	B
M	C	K	I	N	L	E	Y	H	G

See if you can find out the presidents who came "in-between" the presidents listed below.

1. John Tyler _____ Zachary Taylor

2. Herbert Hoover _____ Harry Truman

3. John Quincy Adams _____ Martin Van Buren

4. William Howard Taft _____ Warren G. Harding

5. George Bush _____ George W. Bush

6. Millard Fillmore _____ James Buchanan

7. Chester A. Arthur _____ Benjamin Harrison

8. Dwight D. Eisenhower _____ Lyndon B. Johnson

9. Gerald Ford _____ Ronald Reagan

10. Franklin Pierce _____ Abraham Lincoln

11. Franklin D. Roosevelt _____ Dwight D. Eisenhower

12. John F. Kennedy _____ Richard Nixon

13. Abraham Lincoln _____ Ulysses S. Grant

14. Benjamin Harrison _____ William McKinley

Bonus: Can you figure out what all of these "in-between" presidents have in common?

They were all _____. (*Hint:* Related to one of the two major political parties.)

Did you know that the White House has 132 rooms? That's a lot of space. Many of the rooms in the White House are named either for their color or what they are used for. Several rooms are open to the public for tours during the year.

The names of some of the rooms in the White House are hidden in the puzzle below. See how many of them you can find.

```
F  W  B  X  Y  J  M  S  W  I  M  B  J  L  M  T  W  V  P
B  H  Y  S  T  A  T  E  D  I  N  I  N  G  R  O  O  M  E
Q  B  T  J  V  E  R  M  E  I  L  R  O  O  M  W  L  P  U
D  C  R  M  X  E  V  G  K  Y  L  R  M  L  J  L  W  E  R
U  Y  N  O  E  C  Z  S  R  B  A  I  K  G  Y  L  S  A  V
M  J  R  O  G  D  F  A  C  N  H  X  C  E  O  A  D  S  G
P  K  G  R  T  H  R  B  E  K  S  B  J  M  C  H  O  T  R
R  L  H  E  N  B  D  H  I  D  S  M  L  E  Z  R  U  R  E
E  O  G  U  I  S  C  M  V  Y  O  P  B  L  E  E  I  O  E
D  I  P  L  O  M  A  T  I  C  R  E  C  E  P  T  I  O  N
R  G  U  B  V  H  D  Q  Z  P  C  X  E  Y  T  N  M  M  R
O  K  L  J  F  Y  G  X  D  V  N  T  J  W  S  E  M  K  O
O  C  B  M  O  O  R  A  N  I  H  C  D  P  L  C  V  H  O
M  P  L  F  D  U  B  Y  X  Q  R  Z  M  O  O  R  P  A  M
```

Rooms

Vermeil Room	Diplomatic Reception	State Dining Room
Library	Green Room	Center Hall
China Room	Blue Room	Cross Hall
East Room	Red Room	Map Room

Unscramble the Letters

Change the letters in the starting clue by following the directions below. When you finish, you will reveal the name of the president the clue refers to.

Starting Clue: Served Four Terms

1. Move the F to the beginning.

___ ___ ___ ___ ___ ___ ___ ___ ___ ___ ___ ___ ___ ___ ___

2. Move the T to the end.

___ ___ ___ ___ ___ ___ ___ ___ ___ ___ ___ ___ ___ ___ ___

3. Change the first S from the right to an L.

___ ___ ___ ___ ___ ___ ___ ___ ___ ___ ___ ___ ___ ___ ___

4. Add 2 O's between the first E and the second R from the right.

___ ___ ___ ___ ___ ___ ___ ___ ___ ___ ___ ___ ___ ___ ___ ___ ___

5. Move the first R from the left two spaces to the left.

___ ___ ___ ___ ___ ___ ___ ___ ___ ___ ___ ___ ___ ___ ___ ___ ___

6. Move the S to the 6th space from the right.

___ ___ ___ ___ ___ ___ ___ ___ ___ ___ ___ ___ ___ ___ ___ ___ ___

7. Change the second E from the left to a K.

___ ___ ___ ___ ___ ___ ___ ___ ___ ___ ___ ___ ___ ___ ___ ___ ___

8. Exchange the first E from the left and the M.

___ ___ ___ ___ ___ ___ ___ ___ ___ ___ ___ ___ ___ ___ ___ ___ ___

9. Delete the first R from the right.

___ ___ ___ ___ ___ ___ ___ ___ ___ ___ ___ ___ ___ ___ ___ ___

10. Move the V between the double E's.

___ ___ ___ ___ ___ ___ ___ ___ ___ ___ ___ ___ ___ ___ ___ ___

11. Delete the first two vowels from the left.

___ ___ ___ ___ ___ ___ ___ ___ ___ ___ ___ ___ ___ ___

12. Add the word AN between the 2nd and 3rd letters from the left.

___ ___ ___ ___ ___ ___ ___ ___ ___ ___ ___ ___ ___ ___ ___ ___

13. Reverse the 5th and 6th letters from the left.

___ ___ ___ ___ ___ ___ ___ ___ ___ ___ ___ ___ ___ ___ ___ ___

14. Change the M to an L.

___ ___ ___ ___ ___ ___ ___ ___ ___ ___ ___ ___ ___ ___ ___ ___

15. Add the word IN between the 5th and 6th consonants from left.

___ ___ ___ ___ ___ ___ ___ ___ ___ ___ ___ ___ ___ ___ ___ ___ ___ ___

Electoral College

Can a presidential candidate have the most votes and still lose the election? Believe it or not, yes! It has happened three times already and could happen again. Once the popular vote has been counted in each state, the candidate with the most votes in that state wins the electoral votes. The number of electoral votes a state has depends on its size. For that reason, presidential candidates want to win in states with more electoral votes. In order to win the election, a candidate must win 270 or more electoral votes. (**Note:** This is based on the information used during the 2000 presidential election.)

Below is a list of each state and the District of Columbia and the number of electoral votes it has.

State	Votes	State	Votes	State	Votes
Alabama	9	Kentucky	8	North Dakota	3
Alaska	3	Louisiana	9	Ohio	21
Arizona	8	Maine	4	Oklahoma	8
Arkansas	6	Maryland	10	Oregon	7
California	54	Massachusetts	12	Pennsylvania	23
Colorado	8	Michigan	18	Rhode Island	4
Connecticut	8	Minnesota	10	South Carolina	8
Delaware	3	Mississippi	7	South Dakota	3
D.C.	3	Missouri	11	Tennessee	11
Florida	25	Montana	3	Texas	32
Georgia	13	Nebraska	5	Utah	5
Hawaii	4	Nevada	4	Vermont	3
Idaho	4	New Hampshire	4	Virginia	13
Illinois	22	New Jersey	15	Washington	11
Indiana	12	New Mexico	5	West Virginia	5
Iowa	7	New York	33	Wisconsin	11

Answer the following questions about the electoral college.

1. Determine the fewest number of states needed to get 270 electoral votes. List those states. _____

_____

2. Could a candidate win the election if he won all of the states with an even number of electoral votes? Explain why or why not. _____

_____

3. What is the most states a candidate could win and still lose the election? List those states. _____

George Washington was our country's first president, even though he didn't want the job. Each of the words in the word box below relates to the "Father of our Country." Use those words to fill in the puzzle below. The first one is done for you.

Word Box

two terms	Martha	general
cherry tree	Mount Vernon	Federalist
John Adams	Virginia	

Presidents and Wars

Several presidents have served their terms during wars. Some wars have even lasted through more than one president! Using the names at the bottom of the page, decide which presidents served during each of the following wars. Remember that you will need to list more than one president for some of them. One president will be used twice.

1. War of 1812 _____

2. Seminole War _____   _____

    _____   _____

3. Mexican War _____

4. Civil War _____

5. Spanish-American War _____

6. World War I _____

7. World War II _____   _____

8. Korean War _____   _____

9. Vietnam War _____   _____

    _____

10. Persian Gulf War _____

Presidents

William McKinley	Franklin Roosevelt	Harry Truman
James Madison	Woodrow Wilson	William Henry Harrison
James K. Polk	Martin Van Buren	Dwight D. Eisenhower
George Bush	Abraham Lincoln	Richard Nixon
Andrew Jackson	Lyndon Johnson	John Tyler
John F. Kennedy		

Second in command of the United States is the vice president. In the event of the death or resignation of the president, the vice president takes over. This has happened nine times throughout history. Listed below are vice presidents who became president through the line of succession. Find out which president each took over for.

1. John Tyler became president when _____
   became ill and died after only one month in office.

2. Millard Fillmore became president when _____
   became ill and died.

3. Andrew Johnson took over the presidency after _____
   was shot and killed.

4. Chester A. Arthur became president when _____
   was shot and killed.

5. Theodore Roosevelt became our nation's leader when _____
   was shot and killed.

6. Calvin Coolidge took over for _____ who died
   from a heart attack during a nationwide tour.

7. Harry S. Truman became president after _____
   died from a cerebral hemorrage.

8. Lyndon Johnson rose to the presidency after _____
   was shot and killed.

9. Gerald Ford is the only man never to be elected as president or vice-president. He
   became President after the resignation of _____.

Whether Democrat, Republican, Federalist, Democrat-Republican, or Whig, each has been called president. On the chart below, fill in the name of each president under the political party he served for.

Republican	Democrat	Federalist
_____	_____	_____
_____	_____	_____
_____	_____	**Whig**
_____	_____	_____
_____	_____	_____
_____	_____	_____
_____	_____	_____
_____	_____	**Democrat-Republican**
_____	_____	_____
_____	_____	_____
_____	_____	_____
_____		
_____		
_____		

Did you notice that one and only one president is not on this list? He was a member of the Union Party. The Republican Party was temporarily renamed the National Union party in order to include Democrats from the South who had remained loyal to the North during the Civil War. This president was not elected, but was vice president when the president was assassinated. He ended up being impeached and did not win re-election. Can you figure out who this president is?

_____

Some of our presidents were given very unusual nicknames. To find out these nicknames, cross out every other letter beginning with the first letter. Put the remaining letters in order on the lines below and they will spell out the president's nickname.

1. **Andrew Jackson**

   T O F L A D X H O I B C Z K A O L R Y Y

   ___ ___ ___ ___   ___ ___ ___ ___   ___ ___

2. **Franklin Pierce**

   A H O A S N C D S S I O F M F E D F P R C A K N J K

   ___ ___ ___ ___ ___ ___ ___   ___ ___ ___ ___ ___

3. **James Buchanan**

   U T A E M N Q C U E N N S T G J P I Z M Q M X Y

   ___ ___ ___ - ___ ___ ___ ___   ___ ___ ___ ___

4. **Ulysses S. Grant**

   P U S N G C A L T E B S A A R M

   ___ ___ ___ ___ ___   ___ ___ ___

5. **James A. Garfield**

   A P M R J E G A F C D H T E A R

   ___ ___ ___ ___   ___ ___ ___ ___

   P P B R S E M S Z I F D R E Y N H T

   ___ ___ ___ ___ ___ ___ ___   ___ ___

6. **Grover Cleveland**

   T U T N A C D L D E X J Q U A M B B X O

   ___ ___ ___ ___ ___   ___ ___ ___ ___ ___

7. **Benjamin Harrison**

   D L J I N T H T A L R E N B M E D N

   ___ ___ ___ ___ ___ ___   ___ ___ ___

8. **William McKinley**

   C W L O I B W B M L Q Y B W C I F L Q L L I T E

   ___ ___ ___ ___ ___ ___   ___ ___ ___ ___ ___

9. **William Howard Taft**

   S B L I M G B B W I A L E L

   ___ ___ ___ ___   ___ ___ ___

10. **Woodrow Wilson**

   R P B R I O A F S E X S X S Z O P R

   ___ ___ ___ ___ ___ ___ ___   ___ ___

Some of our presidents were given very unusual nicknames. To find out these nicknames, cross out every other letter beginning with the first letter. Put the remaining letters in order on the lines below and they will spell out the president's nickname.

1. Warren G. Harding

R W A O G B X B Q L Z Y A W B A S R T R D E J N

— — — — — —   — — — — —

2. Richard Nixon

T T O R A I B C L K E Y O D O I Q C T K

— — — — — — — —

3. Gerald R. Ford

Q M E R R N F I D C R E H G P U X Y

— — — — — — — —

4. Jimmy Carter

F H A O E T Q S X H M O L T

— — — — — — —

5. Ronald Reagan

F D A U S T H C X H

— — — — —

6. George Herbert Walker Bush

B P R O G P H P Q Y

— — — — —

7. Bill Clinton

L B A U H B Q B Z A

— — — — —

8. Herbert Hoover

H C B H O I R E V F

— — — — —

9. Calvin Coolidge

W S V I B L R E C N G T E C F A L L

— — — — — — — — —

10. Chester A. Arthur

C E S L A E X G T A R N T T C A U R S T G H O U S R

— — — — — — — — — — — — —

Presidents make many speeches during their years in the White House. Much of what they say is recorded for years to come, sometimes because it was funny, unexpected, or had a profound impact on the way the nation was run. Listed below are quotes from several of the presidents. Try to find out which president said each. You may be surprised! (**Hint:** You may have to think a little bit more to solve these but you can do it!)

1. "I greatly fear my countrymen will expect too much from me."

   Who said it? _____

2. "No president has ever enjoyed himself as much as I."

   Who said it? _____

3. "The four most miserable years of my life."

   Who said it? _____

4. The vice president is the "most insignificant office that ever the invention of man contrived or his imagination conceived."

   Who said it? _____

5. "It does me no injury for my neighbor to say there are 20 gods or no god. It neither picks my pocket nor breaks my leg."

   Who said it? _____

6. "To the victor belongs the spoils."

   Who said it? _____

7. The office of president was "utterly repugnant to my tastes and wishes."

   Who said it? _____

8. "There will be no bloodshed unless it is forced upon the government."

   Who said it? _____

9. "There is no right to strike against the public safety by anybody, anywhere, anytime."

   Who said it? _____

10. "The evidence indicates that the worst effects of the crash upon employment will have passed during the next 60 days."

    Who said it? _____

Abraham Lincoln Puzzle

Abraham Lincoln was the tallest president, the first one to have a beard, and the first to be assassinated. Solve the crossword puzzle below to find out a few more facts about our 16th president.

Across

1. He belonged to the _____ Party.

2. Before becoming president, Lincoln was a _____.

3. His wife's name was _____.

4. Lincoln was assassinated by John _____ in 1865.

5. He was shot while watching a play at _____ Theater.

Down

1. Lincoln issued the Emancipation Proclamation in 1863 which ended _____.

2. He was born in _____.

3. The war between the North and South was the _____.

4. He gave the_____ Address to dedicate a cemetery.

5. Andrew _____ was his vice president.

Where Were They Born?

Some were born in small towns, some in big cities. Wherever it was, these hometowns can brag about being the birthplaces of the presidents. Use the number chart below to find out where some of our nation's leaders were born.

1 = A	7 = G	12 = L	17 = Q	22 = V
2 = B	8 = H	13 = M	18 = R	23 = W
3 = C	9 = I	14 = N	19 = S	24 = X
4 = D	10 = J	15 = O	20 = T	25 = Y
5 = E	11 = K	16 = P	21 = U	26 = Z
6 = F				

1. **Milton, Massachusetts**

   __ __ __ __ __ __   __ __ __ __
   7   5   15 18 7   5   2   21 19 8

2. **Tampico, Illinois**

   __ __ __ __ __ __   __ __ __ __ __ __
   18 15 14 1   12 4   18 5   1   7   1   14

3. **Stonewall, Texas**

   __ __ __ __ __ __   __ __ __ __ __ __ __
   12 25 14 4   15 14   10 15 8   14 19 15 14

4. **Plymouth, Vermont**

   __ __ __ __ __ __   __ __ __ __ __ __ __ __
   3   1   12 22 9   14   3   15 15 12 9   4   7   5

5. **Point Pleasant, Ohio**

   __ __ __ __ __ __ __   __ __ __ __ __
   21 12 25 19 19 5   19   7   18 1   14 20

6. **Omaha, Nebraska**

   __ __ __ __ __ __   __ __ __ __
   7   5   18 1   12 4   6   15 18 4

7. **Yorba Linda, California**

   __ __ __ __ __ __ __   __ __ __ __ __
   18 9   3   8   1   18 4   14 9   24 15 14

8. **Lamar, Missouri**

   __ __ __ __ __   __ __ __ __ __ __
   8   1   18 18 25   20 18 21 13 1   14

Presidential Homes

Did you know that some of the presidents' homes actually had names? Many of them did, in fact. Just a few of these homes can be found in the crossword below. By using the names of the homes given, find out the name of the president each home belonged to.

Across	**Down**
1. Mount Vernon	1. Montpelier
2. Hermitage	2. Monticello
3. Ashlawn	3. Sagamore Hill
4. Springfield	4. Wheatland
5. Lindernwald	
6. Lawnfield	

Letter Scramble

Change the letters in the starting clue by following the directions below. When you finish, you will reveal the name of the president the clue refers to.

Starting Clue: First to ride a train.

1. Delete all I's.

    — — — — — — — — — — — — — —

2. Move O in front of N.

    — — — — — — — — — — — — — —

3. Move second A to front.

    — — — — — — — — — — — — — —

4. Move S between R and O.

    — — — — — — — — — — — — — —

5. Change F to N.

    — — — — — — — — — — — — — —

6. Move D to the third position from the left.

    — — — — — — — — — — — — — —

7. Delete all T's.

    — — — — — — — — — — — —

8. Add J in front of the second A.

    — — — — — — — — — — — — —

9. Reverse fifth and sixth letters.

    — — — — — — — — — — — — —

10. Delete sixth letter.

    — — — — — — — — — — — —

11. Replace the eighth letter with CK.

    — — — — — — — — — — — —

12. Add W in front of the J.

    — — — — — — — — — — — — —

Change the letters in the starting clue by following the directions below. When you finish, you will reveal the name of the president the clue refers to.

Starting Clue: First to fly in plane

1. Swap the first and fifth letters.

___ ___ ___ ___ ___ ___ ___ ___ ___ ___ ___ ___ ___ ___ ___ ___ ___ ___

2. Move the last letter to the second position.

___ ___ ___ ___ ___ ___ ___ ___ ___ ___ ___ ___ ___ ___ ___ ___ ___ ___

3. Delete the last two letters.

___ ___ ___ ___ ___ ___ ___ ___ ___ ___ ___ ___ ___ ___ ___ ___

4. Move the seventh letter to the last position.

___ ___ ___ ___ ___ ___ ___ ___ ___ ___ ___ ___ ___ ___ ___ ___

5. Move the tenth letter to the fifth position.

___ ___ ___ ___ ___ ___ ___ ___ ___ ___ ___ ___ ___ ___ ___ ___

6. Delete all I's.

___ ___ ___ ___ ___ ___ ___ ___ ___ ___ ___ ___ ___ ___

7. Double the O.

___ ___ ___ ___ ___ ___ ___ ___ ___ ___ ___ ___ ___ ___ ___

8. Move the R to the sixth position.

___ ___ ___ ___ ___ ___ ___ ___ ___ ___ ___ ___ ___ ___ ___

9. Delete all F's.

___ ___ ___ ___ ___ ___ ___ ___ ___ ___ ___ ___ ___

10. Add two D's between the second and third letters.

___ ___ ___ ___ ___ ___ ___ ___ ___ ___ ___ ___ ___ ___ ___

11. Move S after the second O.

___ ___ ___ ___ ___ ___ ___ ___ ___ ___ ___ ___ ___ ___ ___

12. Delete the third, fourth, and fifth letters from the right.

___ ___ ___ ___ ___ ___ ___ ___ ___ ___ ___ ___

13. Add the word EVE between the S and the L.

___ ___ ___ ___ ___ ___ ___ ___ ___ ___ ___ ___ ___ ___

Letter Jumble

Change the letters in the starting clue by following the directions below. When you finish, you will reveal the name of the president referred to by the clue.

Starting Clue: Largest President

1. Swap the seventh and thirteenth letters.

   — — — — — — — — — — — — — — — — —

2. Delete all E's.

   — — — — — — — — — — — — — —

3. Add a W at the front.

   — — — — — — — — — — — — — — —

4. Double the L.

   — — — — — — — — — — — — — — — —

5. Delete the R's.

   — — — — — — — — — — — — — —

6. Move the I to the second position.

   — — — — — — — — — — — — — —

7. Replace the N with an A.

   — — — — — — — — — — — — — —

8. Add an F in the second position from the right.

   — — — — — — — — — — — — — — —

9. Delete the sixth through tenth letters.

   — — — — — — — — — —

10. Add an I between the L and the A.

    — — — — — — — — — —

11. Add an M after the first A.

    — — — — — — — — — — —

In each of the puzzles below, each letter of the alphabet stands for another letter. You must break the code to answer each of the riddles. All of the answers will be the names of first ladies. Part of the code is given below to help you get started.

M = A	I = E	C = I	Y = O	O = U

1. This first lady allowed a herd of sheep to graze on the White House lawn in order to help raise money to support WWI.

    ___ ___ ___ ___ ___   ___ ___ ___ ___ ___ ___
    I   J   C   N   B   Q   C   F   U   Y   Z

2. She brought in the first White House Christmas tree.

    ___ ___ ___ ___ ___ ___ ___   ___ ___ ___ ___ ___ ___ ___
    K   M   V   Y   F   C   Z I   B   M   V   V   C   U   Y Z

3. She was the first first lady to ride beside her husband in his carriage on Inauguration Day.

    ___ ___ ___ ___ ___   ___ ___ ___ ___
    B   I   F   I   Z   N   M   H   N

4. This first lady helped create the visitors' guidebook to the White House.

    ___ ___ ___ ___ ___ ___ ___ ___ ___   ___ ___ ___ ___ ___ ___ ___
    D   M   K   W   O   I   F   C   Z I   E   I   Z   Z   I   J   S

5. She focused attention on the Beautification of America by trying to get rid of billboards and junkyards along highways.

    ___ ___ ___ ___   ___ ___ ___ ___   ___ ___ ___ ___ ___ ___ ___
    F   M   J   S   L   C   V   J   D   Y   B   Z   U   Y   Z

6. This is first lady was the very first to have her own office.

    ___ ___ ___ ___ ___ ___ ___ ___   ___ ___ ___ ___ ___ ___
    V   Y   U   M   F   S   Z   Z   K   M   V   N   I   V

7. This first lady helped create many programs to help Americans learn to read.

    ___ ___ ___ ___ ___ ___ ___   ___ ___ ___ ___
    L   M   V   L   M   V   M   L   O   U   B

8. She was ranked as one of the top 100 attorneys in the U.S. before her husband became president.

    ___ ___ ___ ___ ___ ___ ___   ___ ___ ___ ___ ___ ___ ___
    B   C   F   F   M   V   S   K   F   C   Z   N   Y   Z

Presidential Cryptogram

In the puzzle below, each letter of the alphabet stands for another letter. You must break the code to solve this cryptogram. Part of the code is given below to help you get started.

N = A	R = E	V = I	B = O	H = U

V   Q B   F B Y R Z A Y L

F J R N E   G U N G   V   J V Y Y

S N V G U S H Y Y L

R K R P H G R   G U R

B S S V P R   B S

C E R F V Q R A G   G B   G U R

H A V G R Q   F G N G R F '

N A Q   J V Y Y   G B   G U R

O R F G   B S   Z L   N O V Y V G L '

C E R F E E I R '   C E B G R P G '

N A Q   Q R S R A Q   G U R

C B A F G V G H G V B A   B S

G U R   H A V G R Q   F G N G R F .

Eighteen presidents have served since the year 1900. Try to find their names in the word search below. Names may go down, across, or backwards.

```
A  K  G  Q  I  I  B  Q  B  R  T  S  J  E  A  A  B  R  S  W  I  J
Z  T  N  O  J  K  I  G  D  A  R  O  I  F  R  F  B  E  I  K  U  K
A  D  A  B  O  N  L  H  O  L  X  J  M  A  E  U  S  W  W  D  C  N
H  R  H  J  H  A  L  Y  B  R  U  A  M  D  V  D  W  O  R  R  X  O
P  O  T  J  N  M  C  R  Y  X  P  Y  Y  N  O  S  O  H  W  O  E  S
J  F  L  D  F  U  L  R  D  Y  F  Y  C  E  O  Z  O  N  A  N  G  N
R  D  E  C  K  R  I  C  Z  T  B  Q  A  J  H  V  D  E  R  A  D  H
Y  L  V  V  E  T  N  C  P  M  E  J  R  K  T  K  R  S  R  L  I  O
R  A  E  V  N  Y  T  T  P  Z  I  G  T  A  R  P  O  I  E  D  L  J
B  R  S  Q  N  R  O  O  V  Y  D  G  E  Z  E  E  W  E  N  R  O  N
V  E  O  Q  E  R  N  H  I  R  L  W  R  Z  B  D  W  T  H  E  O  O
R  G  O  U  D  A  P  V  Q  I  J  C  H  O  R  B  I  H  A  A  C  D
R  C  R  G  Y  H  C  M  Z  D  Y  B  I  X  E  Y  L  G  R  G  N  N
A  Q  N  H  S  U  B  W  E  G  R  O  E  G  H  K  S  I  D  A  I  Y
N  I  I  Q  E  V  W  K  D  W  S  Y  Q  U  U  Z  O  W  I  N  V  L
W  Z  L  B  A  G  J  Q  C  U  Y  E  E  A  M  L  N  D  N  F  L  K
D  E  K  Z  M  L  A  Q  A  R  U  C  E  D  Z  H  F  Z  G  J  A  K
X  V  N  E  X  O  M  G  E  O  R  G  E  B  U  S  H  X  C  Q  C  Y
A  L  A  G  O  T  E  D  D  Y  R  O  O  S  E  V  E  L  T  F  M  Z
G  Z  R  X  B  P  C  Y  H  T  P  D  Z  X  S  O  R  D  S  W  E  Z
M  W  F  N  T  F  A  T  M  A  I  L  L  I  W  V  G  S  I  Y  V  N
B  N  O  X  I  N  D  R  A  H  C  I  R  C  M  J  C  N  T  C  N  R
```

Teddy Roosevelt	Herbert Hoover	Lyndon Johnson	Ronald Reagan
William Taft	Franklin Roosevelt	Richard Nixon	George Bush
Woodrow Wilson	Harry Truman	Gerald Ford	Bill Clinton
Warren Harding	Dwight Eisenhower	Jimmy Carter	George W. Bush
Calvin Coolidge	John F. Kennedy		

Reading Activities

Andrew Jackson

Born: March 15, 1767   **Died:** June 8, 1845   **Term:** 1829–1837

Andrew Jackson first ran for president in 1824 but lost the election to John Quincy Adams. Although Jackson won more electoral votes than Adams, he did not win the majority. The election went to the House of Representatives and Adams won. Jackson ran against Adams again in 1828 and won easily.

Jackson was the first "common" man to be elected president. The six presidents before him had come from wealthy families. Jackson made his own career in the army and in law. To show his link to the common people, he opened the White House to the public on the day of his inauguration. The people crowded in and Jackson was forced to escape through a window.

Jackson easily won a second term as president, defeating Henry Clay. He retired to his estate in Tennessee, the Hermitage, after his eight years as president. He remained active in politics until his death at age 78.

Use the following clues to fill in the crossword puzzle on the next page.

Across

2. Jackson defeated this man to win his second term in office.

5. Jackson opened the White House to the public on the day of his _____.

7. In his first election, Jackson won more _____ votes.

9. the name of Jackson's house

10. He did not come from a _____ family.

Down

1. The man Jackson defeated in 1828 was _____.

3. Jackson lost the 1824 election in the House of _____.

4. Jackson was a _____ man.

6. The state Jackson was from was _____.

8. Jackson had to escape the White House through a _____.

John F. Kennedy

Born: May 29, 1917   **Died:** November 22, 1963   **Term:** 1961–1963

Use the word list at the bottom of the page to fill in the blanks and complete the paragraph.

John Fitzgerald Kennedy was the (1) _____ man ever elected to the office of president. During the election of 1960, no one thought he had much of a chance. Most people assumed that vice president Richard Nixon would win easily. To everyone's surprise, the race remained close to the end and Kennedy pulled out a narrow (2) _____.

Kennedy's youth and good looks captured the interest of a nation. People everywhere loved to see (3) _____ and read (4) _____ about his (5) _____. Women across the nation copied the look of Kennedy's wife, Jackie.He also proved his ability to lead the nation during the Cuban Missile Crisis in 1962.

Less than three years after he was elected president, John Kennedy flew to Dallas, (6) _____ to give a speech. As he rode through the (7) _____ of Dallas from the airport, Kennedy was shot twice and died less than an hour later.

Lee Harvey Oswald was (8) _____ for the murder only a few hours later. He was never (9) _____ for killing the president because he was shot and killed two days later by Jack Ruby while in police custody.

The assassination of John Kennedy threw the nation into mourning. Almost anyone who lived at that time can still tell you where they were and what they were doing on that day in (10) _____ 1963.

John F. Kennedy brought idealism and hope to a nation. His death brought the end of a dream.

Word List

stories	youngest	November
victory	Texas	family
arrested	pictures	streets
convicted		

Name_____

Herbert Hoover

Born: August 10, 1874   **Died:** October 20, 1964   **Term:** 1929–1933

Solve the puzzle below with the underlined words from the paragraph below.

In 1928 Herbert C. Hoover won 42 of the 48 states in the presidential election. He was a self-made millionaire, and he seemed to be the right person to keep the U.S. economy high. However, on October 29, 1929, the stock market crashed. Investors lost everything and the entire nation was thrown into an economic slump. Five thousand banks across the nation closed and nine million people had their life's savings wiped out. The Great Depression lasted three years. President Hoover did not understand how bad things really were. He kept reassuring the nation that things would get better, but they continued to get worse. Not until 1932 did he allow the government to aid the homeless and unemployed, but it was too late. In the 1932 election, it was clear that Americans did not believe Hoover could pull the nation out of the Depression. His opponent, Franklin D. Roosevelt, won 42 of the 48 states.

Ulysses S. Grant

Born: April 27, 1822   **Died:** July 23, 1885   **Term:** 1869–1877

Choose a word from the word list to complete the following paragraph.

Ulysses S. Grant was the first president elected after the end of the Civil War. The main issue of his campaign was bringing the **(1)** _____ and **(2)** _____ back together after the war.

Grant was a war hero for the North, so many white southerners supported his opponent, Horatio Seymour.

The problem was, many of the southerners could not vote in the election. They had lost their citizenship by supporting the **(3)** _____ during the war. The freed **(4)**_____ could vote, though, and they voted for Grant in large numbers.

Although the popular vote was close, Grant won the **(5)**_____ votes by a wide margin.

Everyone thought Grant could run the country as skillfully as he had commanded his troops during the war. Grant, however, had little idea about what to do as **(6)**_____.

He put many of his friends in important **(7)** _____ jobs. Some of these people could not be trusted and ended up in a lot of trouble. Even so, the people still respected Grant and he was easily elected to another term in 1872. Many people even wanted him to run for a **(8)** _____ term, but since no other president had served three terms, Grant didn't want to either.

After leaving the presidency, Grant lost all of his money in bad **(9)** _____. In order to provide money for his family, he wrote a book about his life and his **(10)** _____. He finished the book only a week before he died.

Word List		
slaves	third	South
government	investments	Confederacy
North	president	memories
electoral		

Gerald Ford

Born: July 14, 1913   **Term:** 1974–1977

Gerald Ford is the only president who was never elected as either vice president or president. He was <u>appointed</u> as vice president when <u>Spiro Agnew</u> resigned the position, and he became president when <u>Richard Nixon</u> resigned.

Only one month after taking office, Ford <u>pardoned</u>, or forgave, Richard Nixon for any crimes he committed while he was president. Some Americans were mad because they felt Nixon should have gone to trial for his part in the <u>Watergate</u> scandal. Ford wanted to put that part of history in the past and move forward as a nation. Ford had many problems to deal with that were left over from the Nixon years, including a high <u>unemployment</u> rate. Few people took him seriously as president.

In the 1976 election, Ford barely won the Republican Party's nomination for president. He barely beat <u>Ronald Reagan</u>, a former California governor. He did win the <u>nomination</u>, but lost the election to Democrat <u>Jimmy Carter</u> in a very close race.

Find the underlined words in the word search below. Words will go across or down.

R	O	N	A	L	D	R	E	A	G	A	N	N	R	T	H	E	W	D	W
S	U	A	K	S	J	P	H	X	M	D	C	B	P	C	G	W	H	K	D
W	U	N	E	M	P	L	O	Y	M	E	N	T	T	W	H	A	L	F	Z
C	J	E	X	X	I	F	Y	M	P	J	O	B	Y	R	C	T	N	A	H
E	D	H	Z	T	T	U	V	J	M	R	O	T	I	E	R	E	G	W	Y
M	F	W	I	N	P	N	X	I	E	S	M	O	C	G	A	R	P	I	D
N	S	M	Q	I	P	P	H	M	V	M	M	R	Z	M	K	G	I	Y	B
Y	P	S	H	P	E	L	V	M	O	Y	M	V	C	P	I	A	R	G	D
Q	I	P	C	G	N	A	G	Y	D	I	Y	V	E	A	G	T	E	R	W
J	R	R	W	G	O	P	W	C	D	U	K	L	K	R	P	E	H	S	O
C	O	Z	Z	M	M	P	B	A	S	C	J	W	U	D	H	R	R	I	W
Q	A	D	L	M	I	O	C	R	I	Q	A	P	J	O	I	T	E	K	O
J	G	W	Y	T	N	I	R	T	K	P	O	G	D	N	W	K	P	E	U
J	N	J	H	N	A	N	E	E	R	A	W	J	P	E	A	I	U	Y	I
K	E	E	H	M	T	T	M	R	Y	Y	J	T	B	D	C	R	B	J	I
M	W	C	K	E	I	E	H	C	B	W	C	C	P	A	Z	P	L	D	C
Q	T	C	S	Q	O	D	N	H	I	L	N	P	I	N	G	L	I	S	Q
C	U	S	U	Z	N	F	P	X	S	V	A	N	B	R	H	M	C	O	G
R	I	C	H	A	R	D	N	I	X	O	N	H	Z	I	I	Z	A	Q	S
O	Z	Q	M	E	R	R	G	U	U	Z	G	H	D	F	V	S	N	A	W

Franklin D. Roosevelt

Born: January 30, 1882   **Died:** April 12, 1945   **Term:** 1933–1945

Paralyzed by polio and confined to a wheel chair, Franklin Roosevelt served 12 years as president. He was elected four separate times. Roosevelt brought the nation through the Great Depression in his first term and won a landslide victory in 1936 to begin his second term.

In 1940, no one knew if Roosevelt planned to run for re-election again. No president had ever run for a third term, but Roosevelt wasn't ready to step down. There was once again war in Europe. Americans wanted to stay out of the war so they stuck with a president they trusted and elected Roosevelt to a third term. Roosevelt had promised to keep the U.S. out of the war, but when Japan attacked the United States Naval Base in Pearl Harbor, Hawaii, he was forced to ask Congress for a declaration of war. The U.S. had entered World War II.

By 1944 and the next presidential election, Roosevelt's health was getting worse. He was elected for a fourth term, but only months later he died at his home in Georgia. He did not see the end of World War II.

Answer the following true/false questions by circling the letter under the correct answer. Then put each letter you circled into the blanks below to answer the riddle.

	True	False
1. Roosevelt was the first president to run for a third term.	W	D
2. Germany attacked Pearl Harbor.	S	A
3. Roosevelt entered the U.S. into World War II.	E	R
4. Roosevelt suffered from polio.	M	K
5. He died at the White House.	R	S
6. World War II ended while he was in office.	I	P
7. He was the only president elected five times.	W	R
8. Roosevelt helped the nation get through the Depression.	I	T
9. World War II started in Europe.	N	F
10. Japan attacked an Army base in Hawaii.	T	G
11. Roosevelt almost lost the 1936 election.	A	S

In what Georgia city did Roosevelt live?

—— —— —— —— —— —— —— —— ——

Born: June 12, 1924   **Term:** 1989–1993

George Herbert Walker Bush was born in Massachusetts. On his 18th birthday, he joined the Navy. After leaving the Navy four years later, he became the president of his own oil company. As a successful businessman, he decided to become involved in politics. He was elected to Congress in 1966 and served two terms. He was defeated in 1970 when he ran for a seat in the Senate. He also served as chairman of the Republican National Committee and director of the Central Intelligence Agency (CIA). In 1980 he became vice president under Ronald Reagan. Eight years later he was elected president. Although he was a popular president, by the time the election of 1992 came around, people were becoming upset by the economic problems in the country. He probably would have won the election had it not been for Ross Perot, a third party candidate who won almost 20% of the popular vote. Bush lost the election to Bill Clinton after spending 12 years in Washington.

George Bush is also a dedicated family man. He has been married to Barbara Bush since 1945. They have five children and ten grandchildren. His oldest son, George W. Bush, was elected president in 2000.

Answer the following true/false questions by circling the letter under the correct answer. Then put each letter you circled into the blanks below to answer the riddle.

	True	False
1. George Bush was president for 12 years.	A	F
2. His wife's name is Barbara.	L	Y
3. Ross Perot helped Bush lose the 1992 election.	G	O
4. George Bush joined the army at age 18.	T	R
5. Bush served two terms in Congress.	I	D
6. He served as vice president under Ronald Reagan.	D	P
7. Bush was Director of the FBI.	R	A

George Bush's son, Jeb Bush, is the governor of what state?

___ ___ ___ ___ ___ ___ ___

The White House

The building of the White House started in 1792. Charles Pierre L'Enfant had designed the original plan for the White House. Unfortunately, L'Enfant's plans were too grand for the new nation and could not be afforded. In March 1792 a notice was put in the newspaper offering $500 to the person who could design a new plan for the White House. Nine entries were received and the design of James Hoban was chosen. It took eight years to build and George Washington did not live to see it finished. Our second president, John Adams, was the first to live in the new mansion.

When John Adams and his wife, Abigail, moved in, the home was still not complete. Even so, it was the largest house in the new country. The White House had three stories and 36 rooms. Abigail Adams worked hard to make the new house livable. The Adams family bought the first item specifically for the house. They bought a large painting of George Washington. John Adams only lived in the White House for four months.

In 1812, war broke out between the United States and Great Britain. In 1814 the British troops invaded Washington and burned the White House. In 1815 James Hoban was hired to restore the White House. Since there was very little left, it took two years to complete.

By 1901 the White House once again needed some work. An executive wing, called the West Wing was added, along with larger bedrooms and more bathrooms. Even after these additions, the White House continued to be in disrepair. Finally, in 1948 Harry Truman and his family moved out of the White House so that it could be completely redone. It was rebuilt room by room and it took three years to complete.

Today, the White House has 132 rooms on four floors. It also includes a bowling alley and a movie theater. Five of the rooms are open to the public. The portrait of George Washington purchased by John and Abigail Adams still hangs in the East Room.

The White House (*cont.*)

After reading about the White House on the previous page, complete the puzzle below.

Across

2. This man eventually designed the White House.
3. The War of 1812 was between the U.S. and _____.
7. He ordered a complete restoration of the White House in 1948.
8. The White House had _____ rooms when it was built.

Down

1. The name of the executive wing added in 1901.
2. The first president to live in the White House was _____.
3. His portrait still hangs in the White House.
4. The room where a famous portrait hangs is the _____.
5. John Adams' wife
6. This man originally designed the White House—Charles _____ _____.

Lots of interesting things have happened in American history and someone was president when each happened. Read the following events below and write who was president during the event.

1. In 1986, during the presidency of _____, the space shuttle *Challenger* exploded 73 seconds after lift-off from Kennedy Space Center. All seven astronauts, including school teacher, Christa McAuliffe, were killed.

2. In 1955, while _____ was president, a black woman named Rosa Parks refused to give up her seat on a bus to a white man. She was arrested because it was illegal for a black person to be sitting if a white person had to stand.

3. When _____ was president, the U.S. celebrated the first Earth Day on April 22, 1970.

4. The Beatles made their first U.S. appearance in 1964, during the presidency of
   _____.

5. Jackie Robinson became the first black man to play in a major league baseball game in 1947. _____ was president.

6. In 1937, while _____ was serving his second term as president, Amelia Earhart disappeared as she tried to fly around the world. She was never found.

7. During the late 1920s, the Marx Brothers began making their comedy movies. Americans were looking for some relief from the Great Depression, which many people blamed on President _____.

8. The Model T Ford was introduced in 1908, during the time
   _____ was in office. The Model T was the first car that was affordable for most people.

9. Babe Ruth hit 60 home runs during the 1927 season for the New York Yankees, while _____ was president.

10. Gold was first discovered in 1896 during the presidency of
    _____.

11. _____ was president when the *Titanic* sank in April, 1912. Over 1,500 people were killed.

12. _____ was president when women finally won the right to vote in 1920.

Theodore Roosevelt

Born: October 27, 1858   **Died:** January 6, 1919   **Term:** 1901–1909

Theodore "Teddy" Roosevelt became president in September 1901 after President William McKinley was shot and killed. He was only 42 years old—the youngest president ever. He was also quite popular. Thanks to his energetic style, his never-ending supply of new ideas, and stories of his fun-loving family, the public remained fascinated with the young president.

Roosevelt was an avid nature lover. In 1902, while on a bear hunt in Mississippi, he came across a small bear cub. He refused to kill the cub. Two days later, a toymaker in New York named a stuffed brown bear "Teddy's Bear" after he heard the story. To this day, the name teddy bear has stuck.

Roosevelt won the presidency in the 1904 election by the largest margin in history. He loved being president, but he made one mistake. In the 1904 election, he promised voters he would not run for election again in 1908 under any circumstances. When his second term was over, he regretted that statement. He was only 49 years old and had many new ideas, but he kept his promise and did not seek a third term. He did seek re-election in 1912, but he lost.

Use the clues below to fill in the crossword puzzle on the following page.

Across

2. This is the state where the first teddy bear was named.

3. He was the _____ president.

5. A _____ named the teddy bear.

6. He was vice president to William _____.

7. He became president in the month of _____.

8. Roosevelt was very _____.

Down

1. The _____ is named after Roosevelt.

4. He loved _____.

5. He did not run for a _____.

6. Roosevelt saw the bear cub in _____.

Bill Clinton

Born: August 19, 1946   **Term:** 1993–2001

William Jefferson Clinton was the first Baby Boomer to be elected president. Before becoming president, Clinton was the youngest governor in the country, serving as governor of Arkansas at the age of 32. He served five terms as governor and then turned his sights to the White House. Although he received less than half of the popular vote, he won the presidency.

Clinton's presidency was one marked by national economic prosperity and political scandal. He helped bring about economic prosperity and growth, but Clinton and his wife were investigated for their involvement in the Whitewater scandal. Clinton was also brought up on perjury and obstruction of justice charges and impeached during his second term in office.

Use the information given above and in additional reference sources to solve the following puzzle.

1. his daughter's name
2. was investigated for involvement in the Whitewater _____
3. number of terms served as governor
4. governor of this state before becoming president
5. number of terms served as president
6. his vice president during his administration
7. _____ U.S. president tried for impeachment

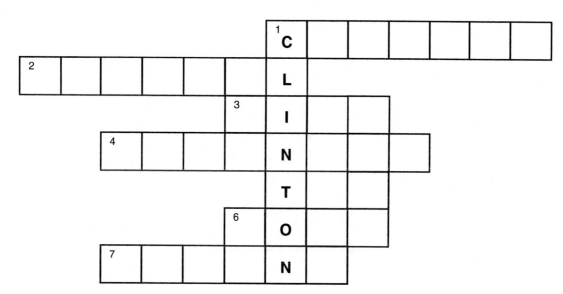

Thomas Jefferson

Born: April 13, 1743   **Died:** July 4, 1826   **Term:** 1801–1809

Thomas Jefferson won the election of 1800 only after members of the House of Representatives broke a tie. Jefferson and his opponent, Aaron Burr, both received the same number of electoral votes. Even though they finally broke the tie, it took 36 different votes to declare Jefferson the winner. Aaron Burr then became his vice president.

Before he became president, Thomas Jefferson had held many jobs, including farmer, scientist, musician, and inventor. He is best known, however, as being the writer of the Declaration of Independence. Jefferson was only 33 years old when he wrote it. He also had an interest in architecture. When the government held a contest to design the president's house, Jefferson entered a design, but he did not win. He did, however, design his own home. It was called Monticello.

Jefferson served two terms as president, and the people wanted him to run for a third term. He declined and returned to his home in Virginia. He stayed busy working on new inventions (one of which was the swivel chair), farming, and studying science.

Use the information given above and in additional reference sources to solve the following puzzle.

1. was vice president during _____ Adams' presidency
2. held this cabinet position (Secretary of _____) when George Washington was president
3. opposing party to Jefferson's political party
4. was minister to this country in 1785
5. leader of the _____ Party
6. his vice president during his administration
7. famous land purchase made in 1803 from France
8. famous home that he built in Virginia
9. wrote the Declaration of _____

George W. Bush

Born: July 6, 1946   **Term:** 2001–

Use the underlined words in the reading to help complete the puzzle on the next page.

George W. Bush is only the second president to have a father who also served as president. His <u>father</u>, George Herbert Walker Bush, was our 41st president from 1989–1993. George W. Bush was elected in the <u>controversial</u> 2000 election. His opponent was then vice president <u>Al Gore</u>. The race was very close up until the end. The election was not officially decided until a month after the voters made their choice. The problem? The vote in the state of <u>Florida</u> was so close that several <u>recounts</u> had to be done before those electoral votes could be given to either candidate. While the votes were originally given to Al Gore, which would have make him the winner, the 25 votes were later given to George W. Bush, making him the winner and the new president.

Bush began his political career as the <u>governor</u> of <u>Texas</u> beginning in 1994. In 1998 he became the first person to be elected to a second consecutive term as govenor of that state. Before that, he was one of the owners and managing partners of the <u>Texas Rangers</u> baseball team.

The following are some of George W. Bush's goals as President of the United States: the improvement of public schools, the reduction of taxes, and the improvement of <u>Social Security</u> for Senior Citizens.

George W. Bush (cont.)

Lyndon Johnson

Born: August 27, 1908   **Died:** June 22, 1973   **Term:** 1963–1969

Lyndon Johnson was sworn in as president aboard <u>Air Force One</u>, the president's airplane only hours after <u>John</u> <u>Kennedy</u>'s death. After finishing Kennedy's term as president, Johnson ran for office again in 1964 and won easily.

Johnson had grown up poor in <u>Texas</u> and he never forgot that, even after he became the leader of the nation. He started many programs to help the poor, the <u>elderly</u>, and young children. Among these programs were <u>Medicaid</u>, <u>Medicare</u>, and <u>Head Start</u>. He also supported a law that said people could not be discriminated against because of their race.

Although Johnson was a popular president, he kept the U.S. involved in the <u>Vietnam War</u> and divided the nation. Many people did not believe the U.S. should be involved in the war, and they blamed Johnson. Because of the <u>opposition</u> to the war, Johnson decided not to run for re-election in 1968.

Use the underlined words above to complete this puzzle.

Presidents' Children

Of our 43 presidents, all but six have had children. The six presidents with no children were George Washington, James Madison, Andrew Jackson, James Polk, James Buchanan, and Warren Harding. The remaining presidents had a total of 89 boys and 63 girls. All of the children were born in the U.S. except for George Washington Adams, born in Berlin; Herbert Hoover Jr. and Allen Henry Hoover, both born in London; and FDR, Jr., born in Canada.

Many presidential children have had government careers of their own. John Quincy Adams and George W. Bush became presidents like their fathers. Several served in the House of Representatives, including Charles Francis Adams, John Scott Harrison, David Tyler, and James Roosevelt.

Several of the children got married in the White House. These include Maria Monroe, John Q. Adams, Elizabeth Tyler, Nellie Grant, Lynda Bird Johnson, and Tricia Nixon.

Fill in the puzzle with the names listed below.

Names

Tricia	Elizabeth	John	Herbert
Charles	Allen	Maria	Nellie
George	Lynda	James	David

George Washington

Born: February 22, 1732   **Died:** December 14, 1799   **Term:** 1789–1797

George Washington became our first president by a unanimous vote, meaning he won every single vote! Washington had been the man who led the country to victory in the Revolutionary War against England and everyone loved him. After the war ended, he was asked to lead the group that wrote the United States Constitution. Two years later, he was asked to lead the new nation. On April 30, 1789, he was sworn in as president at a ceremony in New York City, which was the capital city at the time.

There have been many stories told about George Washington. One such story is that Washington had a set of wooden false teeth. While it was true that he wore false teeth, they were not made from wood. He had sets made from ivory, lead, and gold. Another story says that George Washington chopped down one of his father's cherry trees. This story was made up by someone writing a book about Washington.

After serving as president for eight years, Washington announced his retirement on September 19, 1796. He returned to his home at Mount Vernon in Virginia.

Answer the following true/false questions by circling the letter under the correct answer. Then put each letter you circled into the blanks to answer the riddle.

	True	False
1. George Washington won the presidency in a close vote.	A	D
2. Washington served three terms as president.	F	E
3. He had false teeth.	L	G
4. Washington lived in Virginia.	A	H
5. He fought in the Civil War.	E	W
6. Washington's inauguration was held in Washington.	Y	A
7. The Revolutionary War was against China.	I	R
8. Washington helped write the Constitution.	E	J

Washington crossed this river during the war. ___ ___ ___ ___ ___ ___ ___ ___

Calvin Coolidge

Born: July 4, 1872   **Died:** January 5, 1933   **Term:** 1923–1929

Vice president under Warren Harding from 1921–1923, Calvin Coolidge became president when Harding died while still in office. Harding's presidency had been full of scandals and Coolidge quickly set out to restore the public's confidence in the government. As a result he easily won the presidential election in 1924.

Coolidge's nickname was "Silent Cal" because it was widely known that he was a man of very few words. Even so, he also had quite a sense of humor. A dinner guest at a White House party once bet a friend that she could get President Coolidge to say more than three words. When told of the bet, Coolidge told the guest, "You lose."

After his first full term as president, Coolidge announced he would not run for another term and offered no further explanation. He retired and wrote his autobiography.

Use the information given above and in additional reference sources to solve the following puzzle.

1. his first name _____

2. was the _____ of Massachusetts before he became president

3. won the 1924 presidential election with 382 _____ votes

4. his nickname

5. was vice president during this president's administration

6. Coolidge's vice president

7. wife's name

8. was a member of the _____ Party

Dwight Eisenhower

Born: October 14, 1890　　**Died:** March 28, 1969　　**Term:** 1953–1961

Many people had wanted Dwight Eisenhower to run for president since his role in Germany's surrender in World War II. Eisenhower, however, did not belong to either political party, Democrat or Republican. He finally decided his views were more in line with the Republican party, and he entered the presidential race.

Eisenhower focused heavily on the women voters in the 1952 election. Women made up almost half of the voting population at that time. He also promised to go to Korea to get the peace talks started again. He won the election easily.

In December 1952 Eisenhower kept one of his campaign promises and went to Korea to try to continue peace talks. Finally, in July 1953, the Korean War came to an end.

Eisenhower was a popular president. He ran for re-election in 1956 and won the election by a larger margin than in 1952.

Use the clues provided to complete the puzzle below.

Across

4. political party Eisenhower represented

5. this war ended while Eisenhower was a general in the U.S. Army.

6. the country that surrendered to end World War II

Down

1. country Eisenhower visited

2. month the Korean war ended

3. month Eisenhower visited Korea

5. Eisenhower focused his campaign on this group of people.

Abraham Lincoln

Born: February 12, 1809   **Died:** April 15, 1865   **Term:** 1861–1865

Abraham Lincoln was our nation's 16th president. He was born in Kentucky which made him the first president to be born outside the original 13 states. He never finished school, but he was elected president in 1860 in spite of that. Only weeks later, the North and South were at war and the Civil War began. Although Lincoln did not agree with slavery, he did not believe the government had the right to end slavery in states where it already existed. He changed his mind during the war, however, and issued the Emancipation Proclamation on January 1, 1863. Slaves in the southeren states were set free. The Civil War finally ended in 1865, and Lincoln hoped to use his second term as president to rebuild the nation. It wasn't meant to be. He was shot and killed five days after the war ended by John Wilkes Booth.

Use the information given above and in additional reference sources to solve the following puzzle.

1. former occupation before he became president

2. was the _____ president of the U.S.

3. was vice president during Lincoln's administration

4. state where he was born

5. man who killed Lincoln

6. president during the _____ War

7. issued the _____ Proclamation on January 1, 1865

1	**L**								
2	**I**								
3		**N**							
4		**C**							
5		**O**							
6		**L**							
7		**N**							

Harry Truman

Born: May 10, 1884   **Died:** December 26, 1972   **Term:** 1945–1953

When Harry S. Truman became president, the U.S. was still involved in World War II and the nation had a new president for the first time since 1932. Less than a month later, the war in Europe was officially over when Germany surrendered. Japan however did not surrender. Truman was forced to bomb two Japanese cities, Hiroshima and Nagasaki, in order to bring World War II to a complete end.

In the 1948 election, few people gave Truman much chance of being elected. Truman fought hard, though. He made a thirty-thousand mile train trip around the country, to give three hundred speeches to over six million people. Everyone was so sure that Truman's opponent, Thomas Dewey, would win that one newspaper actually ran a front-page story with the headline "Dewey Defeats Truman." When all the votes were in, though, Truman had won the election.

In 1950 Truman was forced to send U.S. troops into South Korea to help in their war with North Korea. Peace talks began in 1951 but dragged on for two more years. The war did not end while Truman was in office.

Use the clues below to complete the puzzle on the following page.

1. the first Japanese city on which the atomic bomb was dropped

2. Truman sent troops to fight in _____ in 1950.

3. member of this political party

4. became president when Franklin _____ died in office

5. Truman's opponent during the 1948 presidential election

6. _____ for Missouri before becoming president

7. became president while the U.S. was still involved in the Second _____ War

8. This nation was an ally to the U.S. during the war.

9. born in the state of _____

10. his daughter's name

11. one of the Japanese cities on which the atomic bomb was dropped

Use the clues provided on page 59 to complete this puzzle. (**Hint:** Use the information on the previous page and in additional reference sources for help.)

Ronald Reagan

Born: February 6, 1911   **Term:** 1981–1989

Ronald Reagan was born in Illinois. Before he became active in politics, Reagan was an actor with roles in several films through the 1930s and 1940s. His first political adventure came in 1966 when he was elected governor of California. He was elected president in 1980 in a landslide victory over then-president Jimmy Carter. Reagan took 489 of the electoral votes, while Carter got only 49.

Reagan's years in the White House saw many positive changes. Fifty-two Americans being held hostage in Iran were released, inflation slowed down, and the average person was spending more money. Reagan had some setbacks as well. In 1981 Reagan was shot in an assassination attempt by John Hinkley, Jr.

Through all of the ups and downs of his years as president, Reagan remained upbeat and positive. He was the most popular president since Franklin Roosevelt, and he had restored the people's faith in America.

Use the following clues to complete the crossword puzzle on the next page.

Across

2. state where Reagan was governor

4. man who tried to kill Reagan

6. man Reagan defeated to become president

8. country that held 52 Americans hostage

10. position Reagan held in California

Down

1. Reagan's profession before politics

3. Reagan restored _____ in America

5. _____ served as president after Jimmy Carter

7. state where Reagan was born

9. _____ slowed down during Reagan's term.

Ronald Reagan (cont.)

Use the clues provided on page 61 to complete this puzzle.

Richard Nixon

Born: January 9, 1913   **Died:** April 22, 1994   **Term:** 1969–1974

Richard Milhous Nixon won the three-man race in 1968. He won the election partly because of his promise to end the <u>Vietnam War</u>. He was able to pull U.S. troops out of Vietnam, but not for another three years.

Nixon did much to improve the nation's relationship with other <u>countries</u>. He signed a <u>treaty</u> with the Soviet Union to control <u>nuclear</u> weapons. He also made a visit to <u>China</u>, hoping to restore a relationship that had been tense for over 25 years. Because of his many accomplishments, Nixon was easily re-elected in 1972.

Unfortunately, Nixon's <u>second</u> term as president was full of scandal. In 1973 Nixon's <u>vice president</u>, Spiro Agnew, was forced to resign when it was discovered he had not been paying his income taxes. Nixon appointed Gerald Ford as his new vice president. Also, in 1973, it was found that President Nixon had covered up a <u>burglary</u> committed by workers trying to get him re-elected in 1972. Although Nixon was not involved in the break-ins, he knew about them and tried to hide them. Finally, in 1974, Nixon <u>resigned</u> the presidency. He is the only president to ever resign. He never <u>confessed</u> his part in the scandal.

Use the underlined words above to fill in this puzzle.

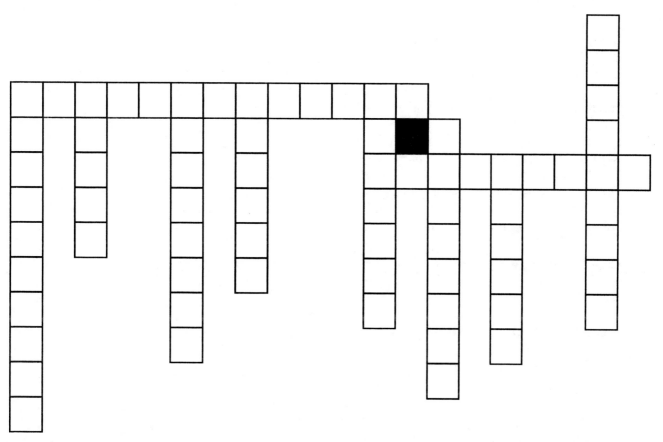

Grover Cleveland

Born: March 18, 1837   **Died:** June 24, 1903   **Terms:** 1885–1889, 1893–1897

Grover Cleveland is the only president to serve one term as president, be voted out, and then be elected for another term. He was the 22nd president and the 24th president. He won the election of 1884 in a close vote and had to work hard to make a name for himself because he was barely known across the country.

Cleveland lost the election of 1888, even though he won the popular vote by one hundred thousand votes. Benjamin Harrison won the election by 65 electoral votes. Cleveland ran for office again in 1892 against Harrison. Once again he won the popular vote, this time by four hundred thousand votes. This time he also won the electoral votes and regained the presidency.

Unfortunately, Cleveland failed to follow through on his campaign promises and was blamed for an economic slump. He left office as one of the most unpopular presidents in history. Even so, many historians now consider him one of the best presidents.

Answer the following true/false questions by circling the letter under the correct answer. Then put each letter you circled into the blanks below to answer the riddle.

	True	False
1. Cleveland was the 22nd president.	F	A
2. Benjamin Harrison beat Cleveland.	I	C
3. Cleveland won again and became the 25th president.	R	S
4. Cleveland won the popular vote in 1888, but lost the election.	H	T
5. Cleveland was a very popular president.	U	I
6. Cleveland served for 10 years.	V	N
7. Cleveland defeated Harrison to regain the presidency.	G	M

Cleveland enjoyed what sporting event? __ __ __ __ __ __ __

Woodrow Wilson

Born: December 28, 1856   **Died:** February 3, 1924   **Term:** 1913–1921

Woodrow Wilson won the election of 1912 in a three-man race. The vote was close, but Wilson pulled out a victory when voters were split between the other two candidates.

Shortly after Wilson became president, World War I began in Europe. He worked hard to keep the U.S. out of the war. Around that same time, Wilson's first wife, Ellen, died. In 1916 Wilson won a narrow victory and began his second term as president. The U.S. was still trying to stay out of the war in Europe. Unfortunately, in 1917 German submarines attacked U.S. ships and Wilson was forced to enter World War I. By the end of 1918, the war was over and Wilson was considered a hero for his part in bringing an end to the war. He won the Nobel Peace Prize in 1919.

President Wilson suffered a stroke in 1920. His second wife, Edith, took over most of the White House business while he was confined to bed. Because of his health, Wilson did not run for re-election in 1920.

Answer the following true/false questions by circling the letter under the correct answer. Then put each letter you circled into the blanks below to answer the riddle.

	True	False
1. There were 4 candidates in 1912.	A	D
2. Wilson did not want to enter World War I.	E	T
3. Japanese bombs bombed the U.S. to start the WWI.	B	M
4. Wilson's first wife was named Edith.	J	O
5. WWI began in China.	T	C
6. Wilson won a Nobel Peace Prize.	R	P
7. Wilson served two terms as president.	A	Q
8. The U.S. entered WWI in 1917.	T	A
9. Wilson served a third term.	M	I
10. Wilson's second wife was Edith	C	D
11. Wilson gave the Fourteen Points speech.	I	F
12. The Treaty of Versailles brought an end to WWI.	C	P

What political party did Wilson belong to?

___ ___ ___ ___ ___ ___ ___ ___ ___ ___

The Gettysburg Address

Below is a speech given by one of our presidents. It is called *The Gettysburg Address*. After reading the speech, do a little research and answer the questions that follow.

Four score and seven years ago our fathers brought forth on this continent a new nation, conceived in Liberty, and dedicated to the proposition that all men are created equal.

Now we are engaged in a great civil war, testing whether that nation or any nation so conceived and so dedicated, can long endure. We are met on a great battlefield of that war. We have come to dedicate a portion of that field, as a final resting place for those who here gave their lives that this nation might live. It is altogether fitting and proper that we should do this.

But, in a larger sense, we cannot dedicate—we cannot consecrate—we cannot hallow—this ground. The brave men, living and dead, who struggled here, have consecrated it far above our poor power to add or detract. The world will little note nor long remember what we said here, but it can never forget what they did here. It is for use the living, rather, to be dedicated here to the unfinished work which they who fought there have thus far nobly advanced. It is rather for us to be here dedicated to the great task remaining before us—that from these honored dead we take increased devotion to that cause for which they gave the last full measure of devotion—that we here highly resolve that these dead shall not have died in vain—that this nation, under God, shall have a new birth of freedom—and that government of the people, by the people, for the people, shall not perish from the earth.

1. What president wrote this speech? _____

2. When did he write it? _____

3. In what war did the battle talked about in this speech take place? _____

4. How many people died in this battle? _____

Ghosts in the White House?

There are many tales about the ghosts who live in the White House. Are any of them true? Well, it depends on who you talk to.

Many people claim to have seen the ghost of a British soldier from the War of 1812 walking around the grounds of the White House at night. Still others have seen former White House ushers and doormen who are still on the job.

The ghost of Abigail Adams, the wife of our second president John Adams, has been reported hanging laundry in the East Wing. Former President Abraham Lincoln's ghost has also been spotted by several people on different occasions, hanging around the Lincoln Bedroom. Some people refuse to even sleep in that bedroom.

Whether you believe in ghosts or not, many famous people do believe in the White House ghosts. Former President Harry Truman said the White House was haunted "sure as shooting." Former First Lady Hillary Clinton admitted the White House was a little creepy, but would not say she believed in the ghosts.

Find the underlined words in the puzzle below.

J	U	N	W	W	D	T	B	I	A	X	T	Y	N	D
A	N	U	H	Q	S	B	O	L	R	B	M	U	I	O
S	A	B	I	G	A	I	L	A	D	A	M	S	H	O
F	B	V	T	K	M	L	P	I	R	G	D	C	A	R
Q	E	F	E	V	S	X	Y	H	U	N	R	V	R	M
J	K	L	H	P	L	M	B	R	D	S	C	V	R	E
M	K	M	O	B	T	H	G	H	O	S	T	S	Y	N
L	O	I	U	G	B	V	T	D	C	T	R	H	T	I
Y	H	U	S	U	H	V	R	F	T	N	O	L	R	K
B	E	W	E	A	S	T	W	I	N	G	X	D	U	K
L	I	N	C	O	L	N	B	E	D	R	O	O	M	C
X	D	V	G	T	J	U	U	S	H	E	R	S	A	C
A	B	R	A	H	A	M	L	I	N	C	O	L	N	F
H	I	L	L	A	R	Y	C	L	I	N	T	O	N	S
B	R	I	T	I	S	H	S	O	L	D	I	E	R	J

Presidential scandals have existed throughout history. We seem to hear more about them in recent years, but there are a few you may not have heard about.

President Thomas Jefferson was involved in one of the earliest presidential scandals. His slave, <u>Sally Hemings</u>, gave birth to a son who was reported to be the son of Jefferson. In 1875 the <u>Whiskey Ring</u> involved a national tax evasion scheme in which 86 government officials were indicted. One of these officials was President Ulysses <u>Grant</u>'s private secretary.

One of the most widely known scandals brought about the first and only resignation of a president. The <u>Watergate</u> Scandal included charges of burglary, bribery, obstruction of justice, and tax fraud, just to name a few. President Nixon was aware of many of the illegal activities, but chose to ignore them. Rather than face being kicked out of office, he resigned in <u>August</u> 1974.

The most recent scandal involved President Bill Clinton. In the 1980s the Clintons invested in a land development deal called <u>Whitewater</u>. The deal went sour and President Clinton had to battle many accusations of wrongdoing.

Use the underlined words to fill in the puzzle below.

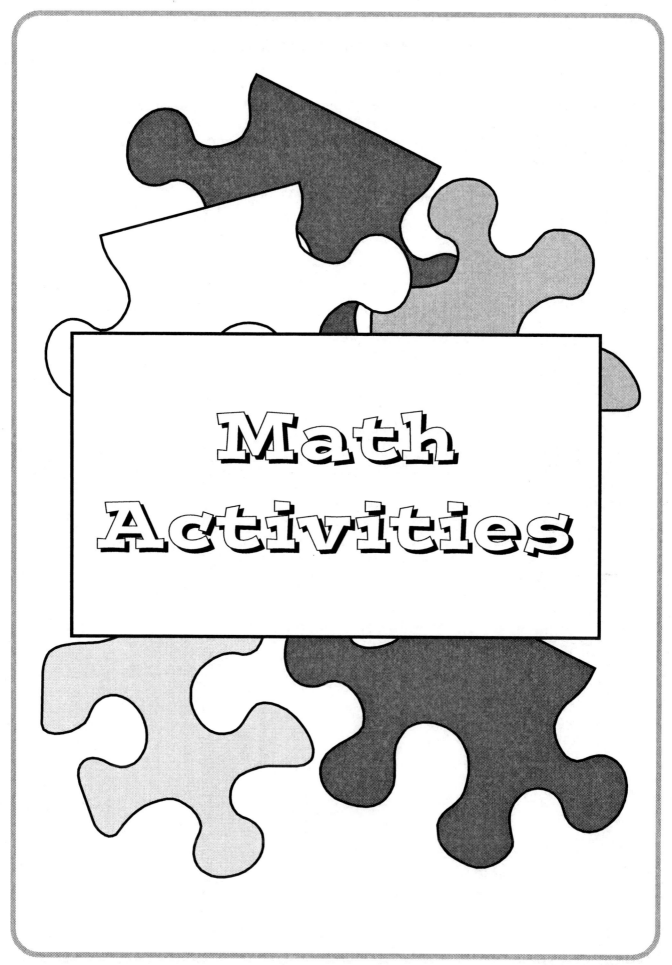

Math Activities

Use the list of presidents on page 6. For each president's name below, write the number of his term (**Example:** Richard Nixon was the 37th president.) Then solve the problem. The first one has been done for you as an example. When you get your answer, find the name of the president related with that number.

1. Richard Nixon – James Garfield = _____ Andrew Johnson _____

   | 37 | | 20 | | 17 |

2. Jimmy Carter – William Taft = _____

   | | | | | |

3. George W. Bush – William H. Harrison = _____

   | | | | | |

4. Franklin D. Roosevelt – Theodore Roosevelt = _____

   | | | | | |

5. Woodrow Wilson – James Buchanan = _____

   | | | | | |

6. William McKinley – Martin Van Buren = _____

   | | | | | |

7. George Bush – Ulysses Grant = _____

   | | | | | |

8. John F. Kennedy – Calvin Coolidge = _____

   | | | | | |

9. Harry Truman – James Madison = _____

   | | | | | |

10. Bill Clinton – James Buchanan = _____

    | | | | | |

Use the list of presidents on page 6. For each president's name below, write the number of his term. (**Example:** Herbert Hoover was the 31st president.) Then solve the problem. The first one has been done for you as an example. When you get your answer, find the name of the president related with that number.

1. Herbert Hoover + William H. Harrison = _____Ronald Reagan_____

   31   9   40

2. Zachary Taylor + Chester Arthur = _____

   ☐   ☐   ☐

3. Abraham Lincoln + John Adams = _____

   ☐   ☐   ☐

4. Rutherford Hayes + John Tyler = _____

   ☐   ☐   ☐

5. Dwight Eisenhower + Martin Van Buren = _____

   ☐   ☐   ☐

6. Andrew Johnson + Andrew Jackson = _____

   ☐   ☐   ☐

7. James K. Polk + James Buchanan = _____

   ☐   ☐   ☐

8. Benjamin Harrison + Millard Fillmore = _____

   ☐   ☐   ☐

9. Franklin Pierce + William McKinley = _____

   ☐   ☐   ☐

10. Gerald Ford + Thomas Jefferson = _____

    ☐   ☐   ☐

Number Word Search

Read the following facts about our presidents. In each sentence is a number. In the word search below, find the word form of each number mentioned.

1. The U.S. has had forty-three presidents.

2. Forty-two men have served as president. (Grover Cleveland served twice.)

3. Franklin D. Roosevelt served the longest—12 years.

4. Eighteen presidents have served more than one term.

5. Eight presidents have either been assassinated or had an attempt made on their lives.

6. John Tyler had fifteen children, the most of any president.

7. Thirteen presidents have been Democrats.

8. Sixteen presidents have been Republicans.

9. James is the most popular name for president with six.

10. Only one president has ever resigned.

T	W	E	L	V	E	B	N	N	P
Q	T	H	I	R	T	E	E	N	D
A	H	C	N	O	F	T	E	E	B
I	B	L	E	N	O	R	T	I	F
S	I	X	I	E	R	S	X	G	I
F	C	A	G	G	T	A	I	H	F
S	Z	S	H	P	Y	P	S	T	T
F	O	R	T	Y	T	H	R	E	E
T	S	Q	D	T	W	O	Q	E	E
P	X	F	L	R	O	W	V	N	N

Who Am I?

Who was the youngest man ever elected president? Solve the following problems. Your final answer will be the number of the president who answers this question.

1. Begin with the number 100. | 100 |

2. Divide by 4 _____ ÷ 4 = _____

3. Subtract 7 _____ − 7 = _____

4. Multiply by 3 _____ x 3 = _____

5. Subtract 12 _____ − 12 = _____

6. Divide by 3 _____ ÷ 3 = _____

7. Add 20 _____ + 20 = _____

8. Multiply by 2 _____ x 2 = _____

9. Divide by 4 _____ ÷ 4 = _____

10. Add 18 _____ + 18 = _____

_____
was the youngest president ever elected.

How Many Years Between?

How many years were between the following presidents?

1. George Washington became president in 1789. Franklin D. Roosevelt became president in 1932. How many years between? _____

2. Ulysses Grant was president in 1868. Bill Clinton was elected in 1992. How many years between? _____

3. Theodore Roosevelt was elected in 1904. Abraham Lincoln's first term began in 1860. How many years between? _____

4. Thomas Jefferson became president in 1800. Dwight Eisenhower was elected in 1952. How many years between? _____

5. Ronald Reagan began his first term in 1980. Woodrow Wilson became president in 1912. How many years between? _____

6. John Adams was elected in 1796. James K. Polk was elected in 1844. How many years between? _____

7. John Q. Adams was elected in 1824. Richard Nixon was elected in 1968. How many years between? _____

8. George W. Bush was elected in 2000. Benjamin Harrison was elected in 1888. How many years between? _____

9. James Garfield became president in 1880. Harry Truman was elected in 1948. How many years between? _____

10. William McKinley was elected in 1896. Calvin Coolidge was elected in 1924. How many years between? _____

What's My Name?

Which president wrote the Declaration of Independence? Solve the following problems. Your final answer will be the number of the president who answers that question.

1. Begin with the number 15. $\boxed{15}$

2. Multiply by 3 \qquad ____ x 3 = ____

3. Subtract 8 \qquad ____ – 8 = ____

4. Add 12 \qquad ____ + 12 = ____

2. Divide by 7 \qquad ____ ÷ 7 = ____

6. Multiply by 4 \qquad ____ x 4 = ____

7. Divide by 2 \qquad ____ ÷ 2 = ____

8. Add 6 \qquad ____ + 6 = ____

9. Subtract 2 \qquad ____ – 2 = ____

10. Divide by 6 \qquad ____ ÷ 6 = ____

_____
wrote the Declaration of Independence

Which President Am I?

Who was the first president to be born in the United States of America? Solve the following problems. Your final answer will be the number of the president who answers that question.

1. Begin with the number 26. | 26 |

2. Divide by 2   _____ ÷ 2 = _____

3. Multiply by 4   _____ x 4 = _____

4. Subtract 12   _____ − 12 = _____

5. Divide by 8   _____ ÷ 8 = _____

6. Add 15   _____ + 15 = _____

7. Multiply by 2   _____ x 2 = _____

8. Subtract 10   _____ − 10 = _____

9. Add 2   _____ + 2 = _____

10. Divide by 4   _____ ÷ 4 = _____

_____
was the first president born in the U.S.

A President's Age

How old must a person be in order to be elected president? Solve the following problems. Your final answer will be the answer to the question.

1. Begin with the number 70. | 70 |

2. Divide by 7   _____ ÷ 7 = _____

3. Add 13   _____ + 13 = _____

4. Multiply by 3   _____ x 3 = _____

5. Subtract 9   _____ − 9 = _____

6. Divide by 3   _____ ÷ 3 = _____

7. Add 10   _____ + 10 = _____

8. Multiply by 4   _____ x 4 = _____

9. Divide by 6   _____ ÷ 6 = _____

10. Add 15   _____ + 15 = _____

You must be _____ years old to be elected president.

Who's Leslie King Jr.?

Which president was born Leslie King Jr.? Solve the following problems. Your final answer will be the number of the president who answers that question.

1. Begin with the number 50.   `50`

2. Divide by 2   _____ ÷ 2 = _____

3. Subtract 5   _____ − 5 = _____

4. Multiply by 4   _____ x 4 = _____

5. Divide by 5   _____ ÷ 5 = _____

6. Add 25   _____ + 25 = _____

7. Subtract 6   _____ − 6 = _____

8. Divide by 7   _____ ÷ 7 = _____

9. Multiply by 8   _____ x 8 = _____

10. Subtract 2   _____ − 2 = _____

_____ was the president born as Leslie King Jr.

Look at the number of votes each candidate received in these elections and find out how many votes were cast in all.

1. In 1832, Andrew Jackson won with 487,502 votes while Henry Clay had 530,189 votes. How many votes in all? _____

2. In 1840, William H. Harrison got 1,274,624 votes and Martin Van Buren got 1,127,781 votes. How many votes were cast? _____

3. In 1844, James K. Polk had 1,338,464 votes and Henry Clay got 1,300,097. How many votes were cast? _____

4. In 1876, Rutherford B. Hayes won with 4,036,572 votes which was less than the 4,284,020 votes Samuel Tilden got. A third candidate, Peter Cooper, got 81,737 votes. How many votes in all? _____

5. In 1908, William H. Taft won with 7,675,320 votes to William Bryan's 6,412,294 votes. How many votes in all? _____

6. In 1924, three candidates split the votes. Calvin Coolidge won with 15,718,211, John Davis had 8,385,283, and Robert La Fallette got 4,831,289. How many votes in all?

_____

7. In 1940, Franklin D. Roosevelt had 27,307,819 votes to Wendell Willkie's 22,321,018 votes. How many votes in all? _____

8. In 1960, John F. Kennedy won 34,226,731 votes while then vice president Richard Nixon got 34,108,157. How many votes in all? _____

9. Ronald Reagan won the 1980 election with 43,904,153 votes, while Jimmy Carter got 35,483,883. How many votes in all? _____

10. In 1992, Bill Clinton got 43,727,625 votes, George Bush got 38,165,180 votes and independent candidate Ross Perot got 19,236,411 votes. How many votes in all?

_____

Margin of Victory

Although electoral votes are what decide a presidential election, the popular vote is also important.

Listed below are the results of the popular vote in several elections. For each problem, decide how many more votes the winner had.

1. In 1824, Andrew Jackson got 153,544 votes, while John Quincy Adams got 108,740. How many more did Jackson get? _____

2. In the election of 1836, Martin Van Buren received 765,483 votes to William Henry Harrison's 550,816. How many more did Van Buren have? _____

3. In 1848, Zachary Taylor got 1,360,967 votes and Lewis Cass had 1,222,342 votes. How many more did Taylor receive? _____

4. In 1864, Abraham Lincoln received 2,206,938 votes to George McClellan's 1,803,787. How many more votes did Lincoln get? _____

5. In his first presidential win, Grover Cleveland had 4,879,507 votes while James Blaine got 4,850,293. How many more votes did Cleveland get? _____

6. In his second election, Grover Cleveland got 5,555,426 votes to Benjamin Harrison's 5,182,690. How many more votes did Cleveland get? _____

7. Woodrow Wilson got 9,127,695 votes in 1916 while his opponent, Charles Hughes got 8,533,507. How many more votes did Wilson get? _____

8. In his first run for presidency, Franklin D. Roosevelt received 22,809,638 votes and Herbert Hoover had 15,758,901 votes. How many more votes did Franklin D. Roosevelt get? _____

Beginning Years

Theodore Roosevelt began the 20th century and Bill Clinton ushered in the end of the century. Fill in the beginning year of each president's term in office on the puzzle below.

Across

A. Jimmy Carter

D. Lyndon B. Johnson

E. Warren G. Harding

G. Calvin Coolidge

H. Ronald Reagan

I. William H. Taft

J. Gerald Ford

K. Dwight Eisenhower

L. Woodrow Wilson

Down

A. Richard Nixon

B. Franklin D. Roosevelt

C. Bill Clinton

F. Herbert Hoover

G. George Bush

H. Teddy Roosevelt

I. Harry Truman

K. John F. Kennedy

Use the list of presidents on page 6. For each president's name below, write the number of his term. (**Example:** John Quincy Adams was the 6th president.) Then solve the problem. The first one has been done for you as an example. When you get your answer, find the name of the president related with that number.

1. John Q. Adams x John Adams = _____ Zachary Taylor _____

   | 6 | | 2 | | 12 |

2. James K. Polk x Thomas Jefferson = _____

3. John Tyler x James Madison = _____

4. Martin Van Buren x James Madison = _____

5. Zachary Taylor x John Adams = _____

6. James Monroe x Andrew Jackson = _____

7. William H. Harrison x Thomas Jefferson = _____

8. Zachary Taylor x Thomas Jefferson = _____

9. John Adams x James Madison = _____

10. Andrew Jackson x James Madison = _____

11. Thomas Jefferson x Andrew Jackson = _____

12. James K. Polk x John Adams = _____

13. Martin Van Buren x John Adams = _____

14. James Madison x James Monroe = _____

15. William H. Harrison x John Adams = _____

Use the list of presidents on page 6. For each president's name below, write the number of his term. (**Example:** William H. Taft was the 27th president.) Then solve the problem. The first one has been done for you as an example. When you get your answer, find the name of the president related with that number.

1. William H. Taft ÷ Thomas Jefferson = William H. Harrison
   27   3   9

2. Franklin Pierce ÷ Andrew Jackson = _____

3. Lyndon Johnson ÷ Thomas Jefferson = _____

4. Woodrow Wilson ÷ James Madison = _____

5. John F. Kennedy ÷ Andrew Jackson = _____

6. Harry Truman ÷ Thomas Jefferson = _____

7. Abraham Lincoln ÷ John Adams = _____

8. James Garfield ÷ James Madison = _____

9. Chester A. Arthur ÷ Andrew Jackson = _____

10. James Buchanan ÷ Thomas Jefferson = _____

11. Ronald Reagan ÷ John Tyler = _____

12. Calvin Coolidge ÷ James Monroe = _____

13. Ulysses Grant ÷ John Q. Adams = _____

14. John Tyler ÷ James Monroe = _____

15. John Q. Adams ÷ Thomas Jefferson = _____

From Thomas Jefferson to William McKinley, they all served as president in the 19th century. For all of the 19th century presidents listed below, find out the year they began their term as president. Then find those years in the number puzzle.

Thomas Jefferson	James K. Polk	Rutherford B. Hayes
James Madison	Zachary Taylor	James Garfield
James Monroe	Millard Fillmore	Chester A. Arthur
John Q. Adams	Franklin Pierce	Grover Cleveland
Andrew Jackson	James Buchanan	Benjamin Harrison
Martin Van Buren	Abraham Lincoln	William McKinley
William H. Harrison	Andrew Johnson	
John Tyler	Ulysses S. Grant	

2	3	0	2	0	1	1	8	0	1	7	1	3
7	9	1	5	2	8	9	4	3	2	8	8	7
6	1	8	0	9	8	3	7	5	4	4	5	4
8	8	1	9	3	9	7	1	1	8	9	7	5
1	6	7	8	7	3	1	8	2	5	7	3	6
1	4	6	2	6	2	8	2	6	6	2	7	0
8	2	5	3	7	1	3	9	7	9	0	6	3
5	0	3	6	1	8	5	0	9	3	1	4	2
3	1	1	5	9	9	2	3	9	2	3	2	5
4	1	8	6	1	0	7	2	4	1	8	4	1
3	4	4	9	4	0	3	1	3	9	7	2	6
7	7	9	0	2	3	4	8	2	9	0	0	7
9	3	4	1	8	9	3	4	1	1	2	0	6
4	6	6	3	0	2	5	5	0	8	3	3	5
0	5	3	1	8	3	7	8	1	6	5	4	0
1	1	0	8	6	4	0	6	3	9	4	9	2
5	8	0	6	5	6	1	5	2	3	7	7	1
5	8	8	5	2	4	2	7	4	1	8	7	7
5	5	6	4	1	5	1	1	4	7	4	2	4
6	0	3	1	3	1	8	8	1	5	3	4	3

Can a presidential candidate have the most votes and still lose the election? Believe it or not, yes! It has happened three times already and could happen again. Once the popular vote has been counted in each state, the candidate with the most votes in that state wins the electoral votes. The number of electoral votes a state has depends on its size. For that reason, presidential candidates want to win in states with more electoral votes. In order to win the election, a candidate must win 270 or more electoral votes. (**Note:** This was the information used during the 2000 presidential election.)

Below is a list of each state (and the District of Columbia) and the number of electoral votes it has.

Alabama	9	Illinois	22	Montana	3	Rhode Island	4
Alaska	3	Indiana	12	Nebraska	5	South Carolina	8
Arizona	8	Iowa	7	Nevada	4	South Dakota	3
Arkansas	6	Kansas	6	New Hampshire	4	Tennessee	11
California	54	Kentucky	18	New Jersey	15	Texas	32
Colorado	8	Louisiana	9	New Mexico	5	Utah	5
Connecticut	8	Maine	4	New York	33	Vermont	3
Delaware	3	Maryland	10	North Carolina	14	Virginia	13
D.C.	3	Massachusetts	12	North Dakota	3	Washington	11
Florida	25	Michigan	8	Ohio	21	West Virginia	5
Georgia	13	Minnesota	10	Oklahoma	8	Wisconsin	11
Hawaii	4	Mississippi	7	Oregon	7	Wyoming	3
Idaho	4	Missouri	11	Pennsylvania	23		

Electoral College Math

Use the electoral college chart on page 85 to complete these problems. For each question, multiply the number of electoral votes in each given state to find the answer.

Example: South Carolina x Minnesota = 8 x 10 = 80

1. _____ x _____ = _____
   Alabama   Idaho

2. _____ x _____ = _____
   Indiana   West Virginia

3. _____ x _____ = _____
   Pennsylvania   North Dakota

4. _____ x _____ = _____
   Florida   Colorado

5. _____ x _____ = _____
   Michigan   Nevada

6. _____ x _____ = _____
   California   Utah

7. _____ x _____ = _____
   Ohio   Louisiana

8. _____ x _____ = _____
   Texas   New Hampshire

9. _____ x _____ = _____
   Florida   Georgia

10. _____ x _____ = _____
    New York   Missouri

11. _____ x _____ = _____
    Illinois   Ohio

12. _____ x _____ = _____
    Pennsylvania   Massachusetts

13. _____ x _____ = _____
    Illinois   Indiana

14. _____ x _____ = _____
    California   Florida

15. _____ x _____ = _____
    Texas   Michigan

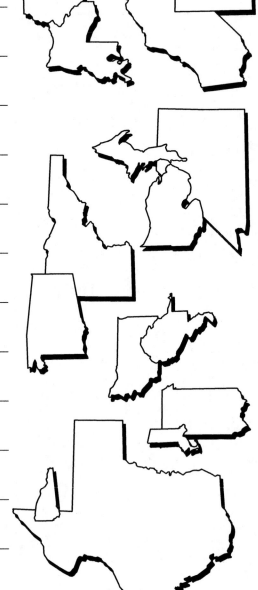

Use the Electoral College chart on page 85 to complete these problems. For each question you must add or subtract the electoral votes for each state given, then find the answer for each problem.

1. _____ + _____ = _____
   Missouri   New York

2. _____ – _____ = _____
   California   Ohio

3. _____ – _____ = _____
   Texas   Alaska

4. _____ + _____ = _____
   Florida   California

5. _____ + _____ + _____ = _____
   Mississippi   Wisconsin   Michigan

6. _____ + _____ – _____ = _____
   Pennsylvania   Texas   Arkansas

7. _____ – _____ = _____
   Illinois   Delaware

8. _____ + _____ + _____ = _____
   Tennessee   Virginia   North Carolina

9. _____ + _____ + _____ = _____
   Connecticut   Alabama   Indiana

10. _____ + _____ + _____ = _____
    Massachusetts   Georgia   California

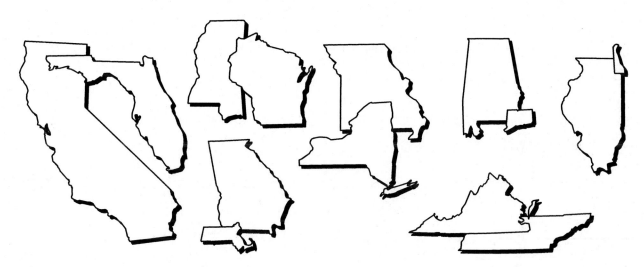

Which State Am I?

Use the electoral college chart on page 85 to complete the following riddles.

1. I am the state with the most electoral votes. Which state am I?

   _____

2. I am the state with less electoral votes than California but more than Texas. Which state am I? _____

3. I am the state with ten more votes than Wisconsin. Which state am I?

   _____

4. If you add New Jersey's votes to Kentucky's votes you get my votes.

   _____

5. I am the only state with an odd number of votes higher than Florida. Which state am I? _____

6. I am the state with ten less votes than Texas. Which state am I?

   _____

7. If you add the votes from Hawaii, Idaho, and Kansas, you get my votes. Which state am I? _____

8. If you add the votes from Indiana, Iowa, and Kansas you get my votes. Which state am I? _____

9. I have less votes than North Carolina but more than Massachusetts. Which state am I? _____

10. We are the only two states with the same odd number between 10 and 15. Which states are we? _____ _____

Work each math problem. Then fill in the blanks at the bottom of the page with the letter that matches each answer. Find the answer to this riddle:

> I was the only president who never went to school. Who am I?

1 603
  – 120 **O**

2 504
  – 351 **N**

3 801
  – 620 **A**

4 905
  – 743 **J**

5 502
  – 241 **R**

6 508
  – 247 **H**

7 607
  – 546 **E**

8 406
  – 142 **W**

9 308
  – 150 **S**

10 306
  – 234 **D**

—— —— —— —— —— ——
181 153 72 261 61 264

—— —— —— —— —— —— ——
162 483 261 153 158 483 153

Presidential Riddle #2

Work each math problem. Then fill in the blanks at the bottom of the page with the letter that matches each answer. Find the answer to this riddle:

At one of my parties, I had a wheel of cheese that weighed 1,400 pounds. It was eaten in 2 hours! Who am I?

1   9
-7 **J**
____

2   7
-2 **S**
____

3   8
-1 **C**
____

4   7
-6 **N**
____

5   5
-1 **A**
____

6   9
-6 **R**
____

7   8
-2 **W**
____

8   10
-1 **K**
____

9   7
-7 **D**
____

10   9
-1 **E**
____

11   10
-0 **O**
____

____   ____   ____   ____   ____   ____
 4   1   0   3   8   6

____   ____   ____   ____   ____   ____   ____
 2   4   7   9   5   10   1

Work each math problem. Then fill in the blanks at the bottom of the page with the letter that matches each answer. Find the answer to this riddle:

My term as president was the shortest of all—only 32 days! Which president am I?

❶ 466	❷ 768	❸ 244	❹ 998	❺ 359	❻ 763
– 225 **N**	– 418 **W**	– 120 **L**	– 516 **A**	– 128 **H**	– 231 **I**

❼ 495	❽ 759	❾ 667	❿ 543	⓫ 498	⓬ 879
– 365 **S**	– 416 **M**	– 425 **R**	– 121 **E**	– 375 **Y**	– 568 **O**

350   532   124   124   532   482   343

231   422   241   242   123

231   482   242   242   532   130   311   241

Presidential Riddle #4

Work each math problem. Then fill in the blanks at the bottom of the page with the letter that matches each answer. Find the answer to this riddle:

It's been said that I wore a wooden pair of false teeth. Who am I?

1 56
− 19 **O**

2 83
− 29 **W**

3 91
− 45 **H**

4 87
− 28 **G**

5 73
− 24 **I**

6 60
− 47 **E**

7 64
− 37 **N**

8 92
− 48 **A**

9 84
− 19 **R**

10 47
− 38 **S**

11 45
− 37 **T**

___ ___ ___ ___ ___ ___
59   13   37   65   59   13

___ ___ ___ ___ ___ ___ ___ ___ ___ ___
54   44   9   46   49   27   59   8   37   27

Work each math problem. Then fill in the blanks at the bottom of the page with the letter that matches each answer. Find the answer to this riddle:

Can you believe it? I was once arrested for driving my horse too fast! Which president am I?

1
23
+ 39 **R**

2
64
+ 29 **S**

3
77
+ 14 **U**

4
68
+ 26 **E**

5
45
+ 35 **A**

6
58
+ 27 **G**

7
26
+ 56 **T**

8
44
+ 37 **L**

9
19
+ 56 **N**

10
31
+ 39 **Y**

‾91‾   ‾81‾   ‾70‾   ‾93‾   ‾93‾   ‾94‾   ‾93‾   ‾93‾.

‾85‾   ‾62‾   ‾80‾   ‾75‾   ‾82‾

Work each math problem. Then fill in the blanks at the bottom of the page with the letter that matches each answer. Find the answer to this riddle:

The teddy bear is named after me. Which U.S. president am I?

1 8
+9 **O**

2 7
+7 **R**

3 8
+8 **S**

4 9
+9 **L**

5 3
+8 **E**

6 7
+3 **H**

7 8
+7 **D**

8 4
+9 **V**

9 5
+7 **T**

___ ___ ___ ___ ___ ___ ___ ___
12   10   11   17   15   17   14   11

___ ___ ___ ___ ___ ___ ___ ___ ___
14   17   17   16   11   13   11   18   12

Work each math problem. Then fill in the blanks at the bottom of the page with the letter that matches each answer. Find the answer to this riddle:

> I was the second president to die while in office. Who am I?

1
56
+ 31 **A**

2
67
+ 22 **R**

3
44
+ 30 **Z**

4
15
+ 23 **T**

5
10
+ 23 **C**

6
35
+ 12 **Y**

7
58
+ 30 **H**

8
82
+ 11 **L**

9
74
+ 25 **O**

$\overline{74}$ $\overline{87}$ $\overline{33}$ $\overline{88}$ $\overline{87}$ $\overline{89}$ $\overline{47}$

$\overline{38}$ $\overline{87}$ $\overline{47}$ $\overline{93}$ $\overline{99}$ $\overline{89}$

Work each math problem. Then fill in the blanks at the bottom of the page with the letter that matches each answer. Find the answer to this riddle:

> I am the U.S. president with the most children. I had 15! Who am I?

1 35
    − 21 **L**
___

2 76
    − 30 **E**
___

3 55
    − 45 **J**
___

4 43
    − 12 **R**
___

5 82
    − 40 **O**
___

6 46
    − 16 **Y**
___

7 97
    − 65 **H**
___

8 77
    − 32 **T**
___

9 48
    − 22 **N**
___

___   ___   ___   ___   ___   ___   ___   ___   ___
10   42   32   26   45   30   14   46   31

Work each math problem. Then fill in the blanks at the bottom of the page with the letter that matches each answer. Find the answer to this riddle:

I was given the Oath of Office on board an airplane. Which president am I?

1
   942
− 129 **H**
‾‾‾‾‾‾‾

2
   356
− 198 **S**
‾‾‾‾‾‾‾

3
   721
− 432 **J**
‾‾‾‾‾‾‾

4
   694
− 456 **L**
‾‾‾‾‾‾‾

5
   367
− 178 **O**
‾‾‾‾‾‾‾

6
   425
− 129 **D**
‾‾‾‾‾‾‾

7
   521
− 123 **N**
‾‾‾‾‾‾‾

8
   743
− 158 **Y**
‾‾‾‾‾‾‾

238   585   398   296   189   398

‾‾‾ ‾‾‾ ‾‾‾ ‾‾‾ ‾‾‾ ‾‾‾ ‾‾‾
289 189 813 398 158 189 398

Presidential Riddle #10

Work each math problem. Then fill in the blanks at the bottom of the page with the letter that matches each answer. Find the answer to this riddle:

> I am credited with inventing the swivel chair. Which president am I?

1
$$60$$
$$- 23 \text{ M}$$

2
$$50$$
$$- 12 \text{ J}$$

3
$$30$$
$$- 13 \text{ T}$$

4
$$60$$
$$- 41 \text{ F}$$

5
$$50$$
$$- 36 \text{ R}$$

6
$$90$$
$$- 54 \text{ E}$$

7
$$70$$
$$- 46 \text{ H}$$

8
$$50$$
$$- 24 \text{ S}$$

9
$$40$$
$$- 18 \text{ O}$$

10
$$80$$
$$- 57 \text{ A}$$

11
$$70$$
$$- 25 \text{ N}$$

$$\overline{} \quad \overline{} \quad \overline{} \quad \overline{} \quad \overline{} \quad \overline{}$$
17   24   22   37   23   26

$$\overline{} \quad \overline{} \quad \overline{} \quad \overline{} \quad \overline{} \quad \overline{} \quad \overline{} \quad \overline{} \quad \overline{}$$
38   36   19   19   36   14   26   22   45

Work each math problem. Then, fill in the blanks at the bottom of the page with the letter that matches each answer. Find the answer to this riddle:

I was elected president by only one electoral vote. Who am I?

1
67
x 4 **E**

2
83
x 9 **R**

3
56
x 5 **H**

4
23
x 9 **A**

5
78
x 7 **S**

6
93
x 7 **U**

7
48
x 6 **Y**

8
76
x 7 **T**

9
34
x 6 **D**

10
18
x 5 **B**

11
25
x 5 **O**

12
53
x 8 **F**

747   651   532   280   268   747   424   125   747   204

90 .   280   207   288   268   546

Work each math problem. Then fill in the blanks at the bottom of the page with the letter that matches each answer. Find the answer to this riddle:

At six feet, four inches tall, I was the tallest of all presidents. Who am I?

1
23
x 6 **B**
____

2
67
x 1 **N**
____

3
34
x 4 **L**
____

4
18
x 3 **R**
____

5
35
x 4 **C**
____

6
12
x 5 **O**
____

7
90
x 5 **A**
____

8
87
x 3 **H**
____

9
63
x 3 **I**
____

10
36
x 2 **M**
____

‾‾‾‾‾   ‾‾‾‾‾   ‾‾‾‾   ‾‾‾‾‾   ‾‾‾‾‾   ‾‾‾‾‾   ‾‾‾‾
450   138   54   450   261   450   72

‾‾‾‾‾   ‾‾‾‾‾   ‾‾‾‾   ‾‾‾‾‾   ‾‾‾‾   ‾‾‾‾‾   ‾‾‾‾
136   189   67   140   60   136   67

Presidential Riddle #13

Work each problem. Then, fill in the blanks at the bottom of the page with the letter that matches each answer. Find the answer to this riddle:

> I was the second president to be shot while in office. I later died from the wound. Who am I?

1. 15) 1290   J

2. 32) 1440   G

3. 38) 2394   A

4. 12) 456   S

5. 42) 4032   D

6. 21) 1176   R

7. 30) 2850   M

8. 18) 1152   F

9. 24) 360   E

10. 19) 551   I

11. 23) 736   L

$\overline{86}$ $\overline{63}$ $\overline{95}$ $\overline{15}$ $\overline{38}$ $\overline{45}$ $\overline{63}$ $\overline{56}$ $\overline{64}$ $\overline{29}$ $\overline{15}$ $\overline{32}$ $\overline{96}$

Work each problem. Then, fill in the blanks at the bottom of the page with the letter that matches each answer. Find the answer to this riddle:

I was the only president who ever published a newspaper.
Who am I?

1 $6\overline{)360}$ **H**   **2** $2\overline{)82}$ **W**   **3** $5\overline{)135}$ **A**

4 $6\overline{)252}$ **R**   **5** $9\overline{)405}$ **D**   **6** $8\overline{)448}$ **G**

7 $3\overline{)207}$ **E**   **8** $4\overline{)336}$ **N**   **9** $3\overline{)249}$ **I**

$\overline{}$ $\overline{}$ $\overline{}$ $\overline{}$ $\overline{}$ $\overline{}$ $\overline{}$.
41 27 42 42 69 84 56

$\overline{}$ $\overline{}$ $\overline{}$ $\overline{}$ $\overline{}$ $\overline{}$ $\overline{}$
60 27 42 45 83 84 56

Answer Key

Page 7

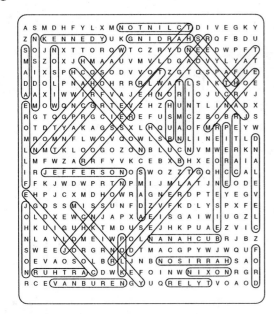

Page 8

1. Lincoln
2. Booth
3. Garfield (across)
   Guiteau (down)
4. McKinley
5. Czolgosz
6. Kennedy
7. Oswald

Page 9

1. D	6. G	11. P	16. F
2. I	7. S	12. N	17. O
3. J	8. K	13. L	18. T
4. B	9. C	14. R	19. Q
5. E	10. M	15. H	20. A

Page 10

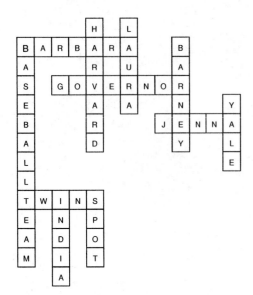

Page 11

Across	Down
1. Roosevelt	1. Ford
2. Clinton	2. Pierce
3. Johnson	3. Tyler
4. Jackson	4. Nixon
5. Buchanan	5. Harrison

Page 12

1. Gerald Ford	6. Abraham Lincoln
2. Ronald Reagan	7. John Tyler
3. Andrew Jackson	8. Thomas Jefferson
4. George Washington	9. Woodrow Wilson
5. John Adams	

Page 13

1. Henry	7. Earl
2. Delano	8. Wilson
3. David	9. Herbert Walker
4. Fitzgerald	10. Jefferson
5. Baines	11. Gamaliel
6. Milhous	12. Howard

The White House includes a bowling alley.

Page 14

H	R	O	O	S	E	V	E	L	T
A	C	R	B	D	U	N	C	X	P
R	T	Y	Q	H	A	M	P	L	I
R	E	R	Y	A	D	A	M	S	J
I	V	E	B	R	O	L	U	N	G
S	Z	T	Y	D	A	A	E	W	H
O	T	R	M	I	P	L	E	F	D
N	A	A	X	N	Q	T	A	F	T
B	J	C	S	G	O	K	Y	N	G
R	T	D	N	O	S	N	H	O	J
W	H	Y	D	C	V	R	S	E	B
M	C	K	I	N	L	E	Y	H	G

Page 15

The Presidents In-Between

1. James K. Polk	8. John F. Kennedy
2. Franklin Roosevelt	9. Jimmy Carter
3. Andrew Jackson	10. James Buchanan
4. Woodrow Wilson	11. Harry Truman
5. Bill Clinton	12. Lyndon Johnson
6. Franklin Pierce	13. Andrew Johnson
7. Grover Cleveland	14. Grover Cleveland

Bonus: They were all Democrats.

Page 16

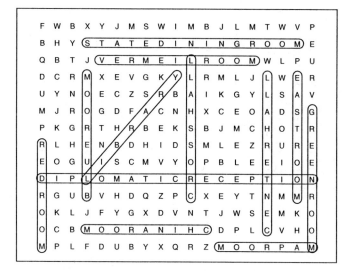

Page 17

1. FSERVEDOURTERMS
2. FSERVEDOURERMST
3. FSERVEDOURERMLT
4. FSERVEDOUROOERMLT
5. FRSEVEDOUROOERMLT
6. FREVEDOUROOSERMLT
7. FREVKDOUROOSERMLT
8. FRMVKDOUROOSERELT
9. FRMVKDOUROOSEELT
10. FRMKDOUROOSEVELT
11. FRMKDROOSEVELT
12. FRANMKDROOSEVELT
13. FRANKMDROOSEVELT
14. FRANKLDROOSEVELT
15. FRANKLINDROOSEVELT

Page 18

1. 11 – CA, NY, TX, FL, PA, IL, OH, MI, NJ, NC, VA
2. No – it would only be 268 votes, not 270
3. 40 – WY, VT, SD, ND, MT, AR, DE, DC, HI, OH, ME, NV, NH, RI, WV, UT, NE, NM, AK, KS, OR, MS, IA, AZ, CO, CT, KY, OK, SC, LA, AL, MD, WI, WI, TN, MO, IN, MA, MN, ID

Page 19

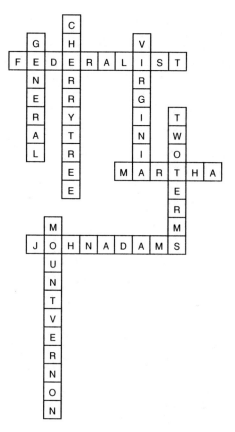

Page 20

Presidents and Wars

1. James Madison
2. Andrew Jackson, John Tyler, William Harrison, Martin Van Buren
3. James K. Polk
4. Abraham Lincoln
5. William McKinley
6. Woodrow Wilson
7. Franklin Roosevelt, Harry Truman
8. Harry Truman, Dwight Eisenhower
9. Lyndon Johnson, Richard Nixon, John F. Kennedy
10. George Bush

Page 21

1. William Henry Harrison
2. Zachary Taylor
3. Abraham Lincoln
4. James Garfield
5. William McKinley
6. Warren G. Harding
7. Franklin D. Roosevelt
8. John F. Kennedy
9. Richard Nixon

Page 22

Democrat: Jackson, Van Buren, Polk, Pierce, Buchanan, Cleveland, Wilson, F. D. Roosevelt, Truman, Kennedy, L. Johnson, Carter, Clinton

Republican: Lincoln, Grant, Hayes, Garfield, Arthur, B. Harrison, McKinley, T. Roosevelt, Taft, Harding, Coolidge, Hoover, Eisenhower, Nixon, Ford, Reagan, G. Bush, G. W. Bush

Federalist: Washington, J. Adams

Whig: W. H. Harrison, Taylor, Fillmore, Tyler

Democrat-Republican: Jefferson, Madison, Monroe, J. Q. Adams

National Union Party: A. Johnson

Page 23

1. Old Hickory
2. Handsome Frank
3. Ten-Cent Jimmy
4. Uncle Sam
5. Preacher President
6. Uncle Jumbo
7. Little Ben
8. Wobbly Willie
9. Big Bill
10. Professor

Page 24

1. Wobbly Warren
2. Tricky Dick
3. Mr. Nice Guy
4. Hot Shot
5. Dutch
6. Poppy
7. Bubba
8. Chief
9. Silent Cal
10. Elegant Arthur

Page 25

1. George Washington
2. Teddy Roosevelt
3. John Quincy Adams
4. John Adams
5. Thomas Jefferson
6. Andrew Jackson
7. Millard Fillmore
8. Abraham Lincoln
9. Calvin Coolidge
10. Herbert Hoover

Page 26

Across

1. Republican
2. Lawyer
3. Mary
4. Wilkes Booth
5. Ford's

Down

1. Slavery
2. Kentucky
3. Civil War
4. Gettysburg
5. Johnson

Page 27

1. George Bush
2. Ronald Reagan
3. Lyndon Johnson
4. Calvin Coolidge
5. Ulysses Grant
6. Gerald Ford
7. Richard Nixon
8. Harry Truman

Page 28

Across

1. Washington
2. Jackson
3. Monroe
4. Taylor
5. Van Buren
6. Garfield

Down

1. Madison
2. Jefferson
3. Roosevelt
4. Buchanan

Page 29

1. FRSTTORDEATRAN
2. FRSTTRDEATRAON
3. AFRSTTRDEATRON
4. AFRTTRDEATRSON
5. ANRTTRDEATRSON
6. ANDRTTREATRSON
7. ANDRREARSON
8. ANDRREJARSON
9. ANDRERJARSON
10. ANDREJARSON
11. ANDREJACKSON
12. ANDREWJACKSON

Page 30

1. TIRSFTOFLYINPLANE
2. TEIRSFTOFLYINPLAN
3. TEIRSFTOFLYINPL
4. TEIRSFOFLYINPLT
5. TEIRYSFOFLINPLT
6. TERYSFOFLNPLT
7. TERYSFOOFLNPLT
8. TEYSFROOFLNPLT
9. TEYSROOLNPLT
10. TEDDYSROOLNPLT
11. TEDDYROOSLNPLT
12. TEDDYROOSLT
13. TEDDYROOSEVELT

Page 31

1. LARGESDPRESITENT
2. LARGSDPRSITNT
3. WLARGSDPRSITNT
4. WLLARGSDPRSITNT
5. WLLAGSDPSITNT
6. WILLAGSDPSTNT
7. WILLAGSDPSTAT
8. WILLAGSDPSTAFT
9. WILLATAFT
10. WILLIATAFT
11. WILLIAMTAFT

Page 32

1. Edith Wilson
2. Caroline Harrison
3. Helen Taft
4. Jacqueline Kennedy
5. Lady Bird Johnson
6. Rosalynn Carter
7. Barbara Bush
8. Hilary Clinton

Page 33

I do solemnly swear that I will faithfully execute the office of president to the United States, and will to the best of my ability, preserve, protect, and defend the Constitution of the United States.

Page 34

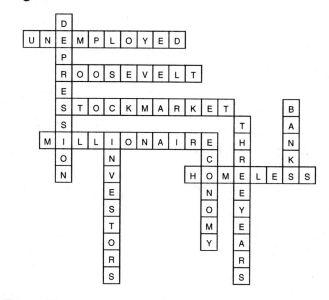

Pages 36 and 37

Across

2. Henry Clay
5. inauguration
7. electoral
9. Hermitage
10. wealthy

Down

1. John Quincy Adams
3. Representatives
4. common
6. Tennessee
8. window

Page 38

1. youngest
2. victory
3. pictures
4. stories
5. family
6. Texas
7. streets
8. arrested
9. convicted
10. November

Page 39

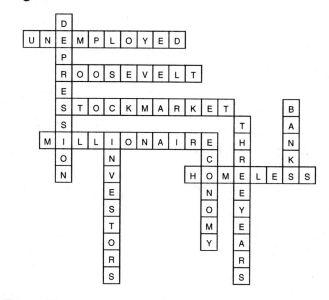

Page 40

1. North
2. South
3. Confederacy
4. slaves
5. electoral
6. president
7. government
8. third
9. investments
10. memories

Page 41

```
R O N A L D R E A G A N  N R T H E W D W
S U A K S J P H X M D C B P C G W H K D
W U N E M P L O Y M E N T  T W H A L F Z
C J E X X I F Y M P J O B Y R C T N A H
E D H Z T T U V J M R O T I E R E G W Y
M F W I N P N X I E S M O C G A R P I D
N S M Q I P P H M V M M R Z M K G I Y B
Y P S H P E L V M O Y M V C P A R G O
Q I P C G N N A G Y D I Y V E A G T E R
J R R W G O A P W C D U K L K R P H S O
C O Z Z M M M P B A S C J W U D H R R I
Q A D L M I O C R I Q A P J O I T E K O
J G W Y T N I R T K P O G D N W K P E U
J N J H N A N E E R A W J P E A I U Y I
K E E H M T T M R Y Y J T B D C R B J I
M W C K E I E H C B W C C P A Z P L D C
Q T C S Q O D N H I L N P I N G L I S Q
C U S U Z N F P X S V A N B R H M C O G
R I C H A R D N I X O N  H Z I I Z A Q S
O Z Q M E R R G U U Z G H D F V S N A W
```

Page 42

1. True	5. False	9. True
2. False	6. False	10. False
3. False	7. False	11. False
4. True	8. True	

He lived in Warm Springs.

Page 43

1. False	5. True
2. True	6. True
3. False	7. False
4. False	

Jeb is governor of Florida.

Pages 44 and 45

Across

2. James Hoban
3. Great Britain
7. Harry Truman
8. thirty-six

Down

1. West Wing
2. John Adams
3. George Washington
4. East Room
5. Abigail
6. Pierre L'Enfant

Page 46

1. Ronald Reagan	7. Herbert Hoover
2. Dwight Eisenhower	8. Theodore Roosevelt
3. Richard Nixon	9. Calvin Coolidge
4. Lyndon Johnson	10. Grover Cleveland
5. Harry Truman	11. William Taft
6. Franklin Roosevelt	12. Woodrow Wilson

Pages 47 and 48

Across

2. New York
3. youngest
5. toy maker
6. McKinley
7. September
8. popular

Down

1. Teddy bear
4. nature
5. third term
6. Mississippi

Page 49

1. Chelsea
2. scandal
3. five
4. Arkansas
5. two
6. Gore
7. second

Page 50

1. John	4. France	7. Louisiana
2. State	5. Republican	8. Monticello
3. Federalist	6. Burr	9. Independence

Pages 51 and 52

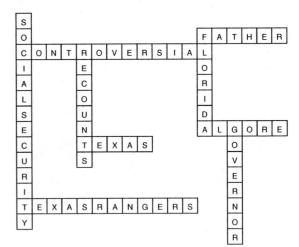

Page 53

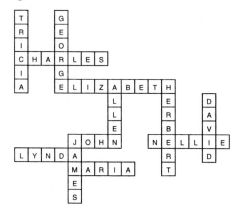

Page 54

			G							
T			E							
R			O							
C	H	A	R	L	E	S				
I			G							
A		E	L	I	Z	A	B	E	T	H

Page 55

1. False   3. True   5. False   7. False
2. False   4. True   6. False   8. True

Washington crossed the Delaware River during the war.

Page 56

1. Calvin
2. governor
3. electoral
4. Silent Cal
5. Harding
6. Dawes
7. Grace
8. Republican

Page 57

Across
4. Republican
5. World War II
6. Germany

Down
1. Korea
2. July
3. December
5. Women

Page 58

1. lawyer
2. sixteenth
3. Johnson
4. Kentucky
5. Booth
6. Civil
7. Emancipation

Pages 59 and 60

1. Hiroshima   5. Dewey   9. Missouri
2. Korea   6. senator   10. Mary
3. Democratic   7. World   11. Nagaski
4. Roosevelt   8. Russia

Pages 61 and 62

Across
2. California
4. John Hinkley Jr.
6. Jimmy Carter
8. Iran
10. governor

Down
1. actor
3. faith
5. Ronald Reagan
7. Illinois
9. inflation

Page 63

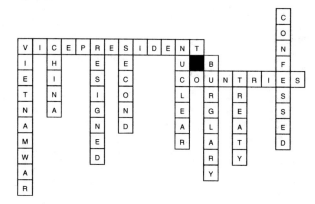

Page 64

1. True   3. False   5. False   7. True
2. True   4. True   6. False

Cleveland loved the sport of fishing.

Page 65

1. False   3. False   5. False   7. True   9. False
2. True   4. False   6. True   8. True   10. True

Wilson belonged to the Democratic Party.

Page 66

1. Abraham Lincoln   3. Civil War
2. 1863   4. about 48,000

Page 67

```
J U N W W D T B I A X T Y N D
A N U H Q S B O L R B M U I O
S A B I G A I L A D A M S H O
F B V T K M L P I R G D C A R
Q E F E V S X Y H U N R V R M
J K L H P L M B R D S C V R E
M K M O B T H G H O S T S Y N
L O I U G B V T D C T R H T I
Y H U S U H V R F T N O L R K
B E W E A S T W I N G X D U K
L I N C O L N B E D R O O M C
X D V G T J U S H E R S A C
A B R A H A M L I N C O L N F
H I L L A R Y C L I N T O N S
B R I T I S H S O L D I E R J
```

Page 68

1. Watergate (across)   4. Whiskey Ring
   Whitewater (down)   5. Sally Hemings
2. Grant   6. August
3. Clinton

Page 70

1. Andrew Johnson   6. Andrew Johnson
2. Zachary Taylor   7. Benjamin Harrison
3. Dwight Eisenhower   8. James Monroe
4. John Quincy Adams   9. Warren Harding
5. Millard Fillmore   10. William H. Taft

Page 71

1. Ronald Reagan   6. Grover Cleveland
2. Harry Truman   7. Teddy Roosevelt
3. Ulysses S. Grant   8. Lyndon Johnson
4. Warren Harding   9. Jimmy Carter
5. Bill Clinton   10. George Bush

Page 72

```
T W E L V E B N N P
Q T H I R T E E N D
A H C N O F T E E B
I B L E N O R T I F
S I X X I N E R S G I
F C A G G T A H T
S Z S H P Y P S H T
F O R T Y T H R E E
T S Q D T W O Q E E
P X F L R O W W V N N
```

Page 73

1. 100   3. 18   5. 42   7. 34   9. 17
2. 25   4. 54   6. 14   8. 68   10. 35
Answer: John F. Kennedy

Page 74

1. 143   3. 44   5. 68   7. 144   9. 68
2. 124   4. 152   6. 48   8. 112   10. 29

Page 75

1. 15   3. 27   5. 7   7. 14   9. 18
2. 45   4. 49   6. 28   8. 20   10. 3
Answer: Thomas Jefferson

Page 76

1. 26   3. 52   5. 5   7. 40   9. 32
2. 13   4. 40   6. 20   8. 30   10. 8
Answer: Martin Van Buren

Page 77

1. 70   3. 23   5. 60   7. 30   9. 20
2. 10   4. 69   6. 20   8. 120   10. 35
Answer: 35 years old

Page 78

1. 50   3. 20   5. 16   7. 35   9. 40
2. 25   4. 80   6. 41   8. 5   10. 38
Answer: Gerald Ford

Page 79

1. 1,217,691   6. 28,934,783
2. 2,402,405   7. 49,628,837
3. 2,638,561   8. 68,334,888
4. 8,402,329   9. 79,388,036
5. 14,087,6 14   10. 101,129,216

Page 80

1. 44,804
2. 214,557
3. 138,625
4. 403,151
5. 29,214
6. 372,736
7. 594,188
8. 7,050,737

Page 81

Page 82

1. Zachary Taylor
2. Harry Truman
3. Ronald Reagan
4. Franklin D. Roosevelt
5. Grover Cleveland
6. John F. Kennedy
7. William Taft
8. Lyndon Johnson
9. Martin Van Buren
10. Woodrow Wilson
11. Chester Arthur

Page 83

1. William H. Harrison
2. John Adams
3. Zachary Taylor
4. Andrew Jackson
5. James Monroe
6. James K. Polk
7. Martin Van Buren
8. James Monroe
9. Thomas Jefferson
10. James Monroe
11. James Madison
12. John Quincy Adams
13. Thomas Jefferson
14. John Adams
15. John Adams

Page 84

2	3	0	2	0	1	1	8	0	1	7	1	3
7	9	1	5	2	8	9	4	3	2	8	8	7
6	1	8	0	9	8	3	7	5	4	4	5	4
8	8	1	9	3	9	7	1	1	8	9	7	5
1	6	7	8	7	3	1	8	2	5	7	3	6
1	4	6	2	6	2	8	2	6	6	2	7	0
8	2	5	3	7	1	3	9	7	9	0	6	3
5	0	3	6	1	8	5	0	9	3	1	4	2
3	1	1	5	9	9	2	3	9	2	3	2	5
4	1	8	6	1	0	7	2	4	1	8	4	1
3	4	4	9	4	0	3	1	3	9	7	2	6
7	7	9	0	2	3	4	8	2	9	0	0	7
9	3	4	1	8	9	3	4	1	1	2	0	6
4	6	6	3	0	2	5	5	0	8	3	3	5
0	5	3	1	8	3	7	8	1	6	5	4	0
1	1	0	8	6	4	0	6	3	9	4	9	2
5	8	0	6	5	6	1	5	2	3	7	7	1
5	8	8	5	2	4	2	7	4	1	8	7	7
5	5	6	4	1	5	1	1	4	7	4	2	4
6	0	3	1	3	1	8	8	1	5	3	4	3

Page 86

1. AL x ID   9 x 4 = 36
2. IN x WV   12 x 5 = 60
3. PA x ND   23 x 3 = 69
4. FL x CO   25 x 8 = 200
5. MI x NV   18 x 4 = 72
6. CA x UT   54 x 5 = 270
7. OH x LA   21 x 9 = 189
8. TX x NH   32 x 4 = 128
9. FL x GA   25 x 13 = 325
10. NY x GA   33 x 11 = 363
11. IL x OH   22 x 21 = 462
12. PA x MA   23 x 12 = 276
13. L x IN   22 x 12 = 264
14. CA x FI   43 x 25 = 1350
15. TX x MI   32 x 18 = 576

Page 87

1. MO + NY   11 + 33 = 44
2. CA – OH   54 – 21 = 33
3. TX – AK   32 – 3 = 29
4. FL + CA   25 + 54 = 79
5. MS + WI + MI   7 + 11 + 8 = 26
6. PA + TX – AR   23 + 32 – 6 = 49
7. IL – DE   22 – 3 = 19
8. TN + VA + NC   11 + 13 + 14 = 38
9. CT + AL + IN   8 + 9 + 12 = 29
10. MA + GA + CA   12 + 13 + 54 = 79

Page 88

1. California
2. New York
3. Ohio
4. New York
5. New York
6. Illinois
7. North Carolina
8. Florida
9. New Jersey
10. Virginia and Georgia

Page 89

1. 483
2. 153
3. 181
4. 162
5. 261
6. 269
7. 61
8. 264
9. 158
10. 72

Andrew Johnson

Page 90

1. 2
2. 5
3. 7
4. 1
5. 4
6. 3
7. 6
8. 9
9. 0
10. 8
11. 10

Andrew Jackson

Page 91

1. 241
2. 350
3. 124
4. 482
5. 231
6. 532
7. 130
8. 343
9. 242
10. 422
11. 123
12. 311

William Henry Harrison

Page 92

1. 37
2. 54
3. 46
4. 59
5. 49
6. 13
7. 27
8. 44
9. 65
10. 9
11. 8

George Washington

Page 93

1. 62
2. 93
3. 91
4. 94
5. 80
6. 85
7. 82
8. 81
9. 75
10. 70

Ulysses S. Grant

Page 94

1. 17
2. 14
3. 16
4. 18
5. 11
6. 10
7. 15
8. 13
9. 12

Theodore Roosevelt

Page 95

1. 87
2. 89
3. 74
4. 38
5. 33
6. 47
7. 88
8. 93
9. 99

Zachary Taylor

Page 96

1. 14
2. 46
3. 10
4. 31
5. 42
6. 30
7. 32
8. 45
9. 26

John Tyler

Page 97

1. 813
2. 158
3. 289
4. 813
5. 189
6. 296
7. 398
8. 585

Lyndon Johnson

Page 98

1. 37
2. 38
3. 17
4. 19
5. 14
6. 36
7. 24
8. 26
9. 22
10. 23
11. 45

Thomas Jefferson

Page 99

1. 268
2. 747
3. 280
4. 207
5. 546
6. 651
7. 288
8. 532
9. 204
10. 90
11. 125
12. 424

Rutherford B. Hayes

Page 100

1. 138
2. 67
3. 136
4. 54
5. 140
6. 60
7. 450
8. 261
9. 189
10. 72

Abraham Lincoln

Page 101

1. 86
2. 45
3. 63
4. 38
5. 96
6. 56
7. 95
8. 64
9. 15
10. 29
11. 32

James Garfield

Page 102

1. 60
2. 41
3. 27
4. 42
5. 45
6. 56
7. 69
8. 84
9. 83

Warren G. Harding